The Best Test Preparation for the

SAT Subject Test
Math
Level 1

 **4th EDITION**

Staff of Research & Education Association

 Research & Education Association
Visit our website at
www.rea.com

Research & Education Associaton
61 Ethel Road West
Piscataway, New Jersey 08854
E-mail: info@rea.com

The Best Test Preparation for the
SAT SUBJECT TEST IN MATH LEVEL 1

Printed in the United States of America

Library of Congress Control Number 2005928374

International Standard Book Number 0-7386-0114-4

REA® is a registered trademark of Research & Education Association, Inc.

CONTENTS

ABOUT RESEARCH & EDUCATION ASSOCIATION

Founded in 1959, Research & Education Association is dedicated to publishing the finest and most effective educational materials—including software, study guides, and test preps—for students in middle school, high school, college, graduate school, and beyond.

REA's Test Preparation series includes books and software for all academic levels in almost all disciplines. Research & Education Association publishes test preps for students who have not yet entered high school, as well as high school students preparing to enter college. Students from countries around the world seeking to attend college in the United States will find the assistance they need in REA's publications. For college students seeking advanced degrees, REA publishes test preps for many major graduate school admission examinations in a wide variety of disciplines, including engineering, law, and medicine. Students at every level, in every field, with every ambition can find what they are looking for among REA's publications.

REA's practice tests are always based upon the most recently administered exams, and include every type of question that you can expect on the actual exams.

REA's publications and educational materials are highly regarded and continually receive an unprecedented amount of praise from professionals, instructors, librarians, parents, and students. Our authors are as diverse as the fields represented in the books we publish. They are well-known in their respective disciplines and serve on the faculties of prestigious high schools, colleges, and universities throughout the United States and Canada.

Today, REA's wide-ranging catalog is a leading resource for teachers, students, and professionals.

We invite you to visit us at *www.rea.com* to find out how "REA is making the world smarter."

STAFF ACKNOWLEDGMENTS

We would like to thank Larry B. Kling, Vice President, Editorial, for his overall guidance; Pam Weston, Vice President, Publishing, for setting the quality standards for production integrity and managing the publication to completion; Kristin Massaro for editorial contributions; Diane Goldschmidt, Associate Editor, for post-production quality assurance; and Christine Saul, Senior Graphic Designer, for designing our cover.

THE SAT SUBJECT TEST IN

Math
Level 1

CHAPTER 1
About the Test

Chapter 1

ABOUT THE TEST

ABOUT THIS BOOK

This book provides you with an accurate and complete representation of the SAT Math Level 1 Subject Test. Inside you will find a complete course review designed to provide you with the information and strategies needed to do well on the exam, as well as six practice tests based on the actual exam. The practice tests contain every type of question that you can expect to appear on the SAT Math Level 1 Subject Test. Following each test you will find an answer key with detailed explanations designed to help you master the test material.

ABOUT THE TEST

Who Takes the Test and What Is It Used for?

Students planning to attend college take the SAT Math Level 1 Subject Test for one of two reasons:

(1) Because it's an admission requirement of the college or university to which they are applying,

or

(2) To demonstrate proficiency in Mathematics.

The SAT Math Level 1 exam is designed for students who have taken more than three years of college preparatory mathematics (two years of algebra and a year of geometry).

Who Administers the Test?

The SAT Math Level 1 Subject Test is developed by the College Board and administered by Educational Testing Service (ETS). The test development process involves the assistance of educators throughout the country, and is designed and implemented to ensure that the content and difficulty level of the test are appropriate.

When Should the SAT Math Level 1 be Taken?

If you are applying to a college that requires Subject Test scores as part of the admissions process, you should take the SAT Math Level 1 Subject Test by November or January of your senior year. If your scores are being used only for placement purposes, you may be able to take the test in the spring. Make sure to contact the colleges to which you are applying for more specific information.

When and Where is the Test Given?

The SAT Math Level 1 Subject Test is administered five times a year at many locations throughout the country, mostly high schools. The test is given in November, December, January, May, and June.

To receive information on upcoming administrations of the exam, consult the publication *Taking the SAT Subject Tests,* which may be obtained from your guidance counselor or by contacting:

> College Board SAT Program
> P.O. Box 6200
> Princeton, NJ 08541–6200
> Phone: (609) 771-7600
> Website: www.collegeboard.org

Is there a Registration Fee?

You must pay a registration fee to take the SAT Math Level 1. Consult the publication *Taking the SAT Subject Tests* for information on the fee structure. Financial assistance may be granted in certain situations. To find out if you qualify and to register for assistance, contact your academic advisor.

What Kind of Calculator Can I Use?

Your calculator should be, at the minimum, a scientific calculator. It can be programmable or non-programmable. Bear in mind, however, that for perhaps 60 percent of the test items, the calculator will afford you no advantage and, moreover, may actually work against you. No pocket organizers, hand-held minicomputers, paper tape, or noisy calculators may be used. In addition, no calculator requiring an external power source will be allowed. Finally, no sharing of calculators will be permitted—you must bring your own.

Make sure you are thoroughly familiar with the operation of your calculator before the test. Your performance on the test could suffer if you spend too much time searching for the correct function on your calculator.

HOW TO USE THIS BOOK

What Do I Study First?

Remember that the SAT Math Level 1 Subject Test is designed to test knowledge that has been acquired throughout your education. Therefore, the best way to prepare for the exam is to refresh yourself by thoroughly studying our review material and taking the sample tests provided in this book. They will familiarize you with the types of questions, directions, and format of the SAT Math Level 1 Subject Test.

To begin your studies, read over the reviews and the suggestions for test-taking, take one of the practice tests to determine your area(s) of weakness, and then restudy the review material, focusing on your specific problem areas. The course review includes the information you need to know when taking the exam. Make sure to take the remaining practice tests to further test yourself and become familiar with the format of the SAT Math Level 1 Subject Test.

When Should I Start Studying?

It is never too early to start studying for the SAT Math Level 1 test. The earlier you begin, the more time you will have to sharpen your skills. Do not procrastinate! Cramming is *not* an effective way to study, since it does not allow you the time needed to learn the test material. The sooner you learn the format of the exam, the more comfortable you will be when you take it.

FORMAT OF THE SAT MATH LEVEL 1

The Math Level 1 is a one-hour exam consisting of 50 multiple-choice questions. Each question has five possible answer choices, lettered (A) through (E).

Material Tested

The following table summarizes the distribution of topics covered on the SAT Math Level 1 exam:

Topic	Percentage of Test	Number of Questions
Algebra	30	15
Geometry	20	10
Solid Geometry	6	3
Coordinate Geometry	12	6
Trigonomtetry	8	4
Functions	12	6
Statistics	6	3
Miscellaneous	6	3

*Includes logic and proof, elementary number theory, sequences, and limits.

The questions on the Math 1 are grouped into three larger categories, according to whether or not you need to use your calculator:

Category	Definition	Approxomate Percentage of Questions
Calculator Inactive	Calculator not necessary or advantageous	60
Calculator Neutral	Calculator may be useful, but not absolutely necessary	40
Calculator Active	Calculator is necessary to solve the problem	

SCORING THE SAT MATH LEVEL 1

The SAT Math Level 1 Test, like all other Subject Tests, is scored on a 200-800 scale.

How Do I Score My Practice Test?

Your exam is scored by crediting one point for each correct answer and deducting one-fourth of a point for each incorrect answer. There is no deduction for answers that are omitted. Use the worksheets below to calculate your raw score and to record your scores for the six practice tests.

SCORING WORKSHEET

_____ — (_____ X 1/4) = _____
number correct   number incorrect   Raw Score
                    (do not include   (round to nearest
                    unanswered questions)   whole point)

	Raw Score	**Scaled Score**
Test 1	_____	_____
Test 2	_____	_____
Test 3	_____	_____
Test 4	_____	_____
Test 5	_____	_____
Test 6	_____	_____

Calculating Your Scaled Score

Scores on the SAT Math Level 1 Subject Test range from 200 to 800. This table shows you how to convert your raw score to a scaled score*.

SCORE CONVERSION TABLE

Raw Score	Scaled Score	Raw Score	Scaled Score
50	800	18	490
49	790	17	480
48	780	16	470
47	780	15	460
46	770	14	460
45	750	13	450
44	740	12	440
43	740	11	430
42	730	10	420
41	720	9	420
40	710	8	410
39	710	7	400
38	700	6	390
37	690	5	380
36	680	4	380
35	670	3	370
34	660	2	360
33	650	1	350
32	640	0	340
31	630	-1	340
30	620	-2	330
29	600	-3	320
28	590	-4	310
27	580	-5	300
26	570	-6	300
25	560	-7	280
24	550	-8	270
23	540	-9	260
22	530	-10	260
21	520	-11	250
20	510	-12	240
19	500		

* **The scores you achieve on our practice tests will strongly *approximate* your performance on the SAT Math Level 1. Strict correlations cannot be assumed.**

STUDYING FOR THE SAT MATH LEVEL 1

It is very important to choose the time and place for studying that works best for you. Some students may set aside a certain number of hours every morning to study, while others may choose to study at night before going to sleep. Other students may study during the day, while waiting on a line, or even while eating lunch. Only you can determine when and where your study time will be most effective. Be consistent and use your time wisely. Work out a study routine and stick to it!

When you take the practice tests, try to make your testing conditions as much like the actual test as possible. Turn your television and radio off, and sit down at a quiet table free from distraction. Make sure to time yourself with a timer.

As you complete each practice test, score your test and thoroughly review the explanations to the questions you answered incorrectly; however, do not review too much at any one time. Concentrate on one problem area at a time by reviewing the questions and explanations, and by studying our review until you are confident you completely understand the material.

Keep track of your scores. By doing so, you will be able to gauge your progress and discover general weaknesses in particular sections. You should carefully study the reviews that cover your areas of difficulty, as this will build your skills in those areas.

TEST-TAKING TIPS

Although you may be unfamiliar with standardized tests such as the SAT Math Level 1 Subject Test, there are many ways to acquaint yourself with this type of examination and help alleviate your test-taking anxieties. Listed below are ways to help you become accustomed to the SAT Math Level 1 Subject Test, some of which may apply to other standardized tests as well.

Become comfortable with the format of the exam. When you are practicing to take the SAT Math Level 1 Subject Test, simulate the conditions under which you will be taking the actual test. Stay calm and pace yourself. After simulating the test only a couple of times, you will boost your chances of doing well, and you will be able to sit down for the actual exam with much more confidence.

Know the directions and format for each section of the test. Familiarizing yourself with the directions and format of the exam will not only save you time, but will also ensure that you are familiar enough with the SAT Math Level 1 Subject Test to avoid nervousness (and the mistakes caused by being nervous).

Do your scratchwork in the margins of the test booklet. You will not be given scrap paper during the exam, and you may not perform scratchwork on your answer sheet. Space is provided in your test booklet to do any necessary work or draw diagrams.

If you are unsure of an answer, guess. However—if you do guess, guess wisely. Use the process of elimination by going through each answer to a question and ruling out as many of the answer choices as possible. By eliminating three answer choices, you give yourself a fifty-fifty chance of answering correctly since there will only be two choices left from which to make your guess.

Mark your answers in the appropriate spaces on the answer sheet. Each numbered row will contain five ovals corresponding to each answer choice for that question. Fill in the circle that corresponds to your answer darkly, completely, and neatly. You can change your answer, but remember to completely erase your old answer. Any stray lines or unnecessary marks may cause the machine to score your answer incorrectly. When you have finished working on a section, you may want to go back and check to make sure your answers correspond to the correct questions. Marking one answer in the wrong space will throw off the rest of your test, whether it is graded by machine or by hand.

You don't have to answer every question. You are not penalized if you do not answer every question. The only penalty you receive is if you answer a question incorrectly. Try to use the guessing strategy, but if you are truly stumped by a question, you do not have to answer it.

Work quickly and steadily. You have a limited amount of time to work on each section, so you need to work quickly and steadily. Avoid focusing on one problem for too long. Taking the practice tests in this book will help you to learn how to budget your time.

Before the Test

Make sure you know where your test center is well in advance of your test day so you do not get lost on the day of the test. On the night before the test, gather together the materials you will need the next day:

- Your admission ticket
- Two forms of identification (e.g., driver's license, student identification card, or current alien registration card)
- Two No. 2 pencils with erasers
- Your calculator
- Directions to the test center
- A watch (if you wish) but not one that makes noise, as it may disturb other test-takers

On the day of the test, you should wake up early (it is hoped after a decent night's rest) and have a good breakfast. Dress comfortably, so that you are not distracted by being too hot or too cold while taking the test. Also, plan to arrive at the test center early. This will allow you to collect your thoughts and relax before the test, and will also spare you the stress of being late. If you arrive after the test begins, you will not be admitted and you will not receive a refund.

During the Test

When you arrive at the test center, try to find a seat where you feel you will be comfortable. Follow all the rules and instructions given by the test supervisor. If you do not, you risk being dismissed from the test and having your scores canceled.

Once all the test materials are passed out, the test instructor will give you directions for filling out your answer sheet. Fill this sheet out carefully since this information will appear on your score report.

After the Test

When you have completed the SAT Math Level 1 Subject Test, you may hand in your test materials and leave. Then, go home and relax

When Will I Receive My Score Report and What Will It Look Like?

You should receive your score report about five weeks after you take the test. This report will include your scores, percentile ranks, and interpretive information.

THE SAT SUBJECT TEST IN

Math
Level 1

CHAPTER 2
Course Review

Chapter 2

COURSE REVIEW

ALGEBRAIC LAWS AND OPERATIONS

Addition, Subtraction, Multiplication, and Division

To add two numbers with like signs, add their absolute values and prefix the sums with the common sign.

Example:

$$-2 + (-3) = -5$$

To add two numbers with unlike signs, find the difference between their absolute values, and prefix the result with the sign of the number with the greater absolute value.

Example:

$$-5 + 2 = -3$$

To subtract a negative number b from another number a, change the sign of b and add to a.

Example:

$$-2 - (-3) = -2 + 3 = 1$$

To multiply (or divide) two numbers having like signs, multiply (or divide) their absolute values and prefix the result with a positive sign.

Example:

$$(-2)(-3) = 6$$

To multiply (or divide) two numbers having unlike signs, multiply (or divide) their absolute values and prefix the result with a negative sign.

Example:

$$6 \div (-2) = -3.$$

Operations with Fractions

The value of a fraction remains unchanged if its numerator and denominator are both multiplied or divided by the same number, other than zero.

Example:

$$\frac{1}{2}\left(\frac{2}{2}\right) = \frac{2}{4} \quad \text{and} \quad \frac{x}{z}\frac{y}{y} = \frac{xy}{zy}$$

The sum of fractions having a common denominator is a fraction whose numerator is the algebraic sum of the numerators of the given fractions and whose denominator is the common denominator.

Example:

$$\frac{2}{7} + \frac{3}{7} = \frac{5}{7} \quad \text{and} \quad \frac{x}{z} + \frac{y}{z} = \frac{x+y}{z}$$

To find the sum of two fractions having different denominators, find the lowest common denominator of the different denominators. Then convert the fractions into equivalent fractions having the lowest common denominator as a denominator.

Example:

$$\frac{1}{4} + \frac{3}{5} = \frac{1(5)}{4(5)} + \frac{3(4)}{5(4)} = \frac{17}{20} \quad \text{and} \quad \frac{a}{x} + \frac{b}{y} = \frac{ay}{xy} + \frac{bx}{yx} = \frac{ay+bx}{xy}$$

The product of two or more fractions is a fraction whose numerator is the product of the numerators of the given fractions and whose denominator is the product of the denominators of the given fractions.

Example:

$$\frac{3}{5}\left(\frac{4}{7}\right) = \frac{12}{35} \quad \text{and} \quad \frac{a}{x}\frac{b}{y} = \frac{ab}{xy}$$

The quotient of two fractions is obtained by inverting the divisor and then multiplying.

Example:

$$\frac{3}{5} \div \frac{4}{7} = \frac{3}{5}\left(\frac{7}{4}\right) = \frac{21}{20} \quad \text{and} \quad \frac{a}{x} \div \frac{b}{y} = \frac{a}{x}\frac{y}{b} = \frac{ay}{xb}$$

Base, Exponent, and Power

Given the expression $a^n = b$, a is called the base and n is called the exponent or power.

Definitions:

$$a^0 = 1, \text{ if } a \neq 0$$

$$a^{-n} = \frac{1}{a^n}$$

$$a^{m/n} = \sqrt[n]{a^m}$$

Properties of Exponents:

$$a^p a^q = a^{p+q}$$

$$(a^p)^q = a^{pq}$$

$$\frac{a^p}{a^q} = a^{p-q}$$

$$(ab)^p = a^p b^p$$

$$\left(\frac{a}{b}\right)^p = \frac{a^p}{b^p}$$

Roots and Radicals

Definition:

If n is a positive odd number, then $\sqrt[n]{a}$ is the number, x, such that $x^n = a$. If n is a positive even number, then $\sqrt[n]{a}$ is the non-negative number x such that $x^n = a$.

$$a = \sqrt{a^2}$$

Properties of radicals:

$$\sqrt[n]{ab} = \sqrt[n]{a}\sqrt[n]{b}$$

$$\sqrt[n]{a/b} = \frac{\sqrt[n]{a}}{\sqrt[n]{b}}$$

$$\sqrt[n]{a^m} = \left(\sqrt[n]{a}\right)^m$$

$$\sqrt[m]{\sqrt[n]{a}} = \sqrt[mn]{a}$$

Absolute Value

Definition:

$$|a| = \begin{cases} a \text{ if } a \geq 0 \\ -a \text{ if } a < 0 \end{cases}$$

Equivalently, the distance on the number line from a to 0 is the absolute value of a.

Properties of absolute value:

$$|-a| = |a|$$

$$|a| \geq 0, \text{ equality holding if and only if } a = 0$$

$$\left|\frac{a}{b}\right| = \frac{|a|}{|b|}$$

$$|ab| = |a||b|$$

$$|a|^2 = a^2$$

Complex Numbers

A complex number is of the form $a + bi$ where a and b are constants, $b \neq 0$, and $i^2 = -1$.

To add, subtract, or multiply complex numbers, compute in the usual way, replace i^2 with -1, and simplify.

$$(a + bi) + (c + di) = (a + c) + (b + d)i$$
$$(a + bi) - (c + di) = (a - c) + (b - d)i$$
$$(a + bi)(c + di) = ac + adi + bci + bdi^2 = ac - bd + (ad + bc)i$$

POLYNOMIALS

Linear Equations and Inequalities

Definition:

A **linear equation** in one variable is one that can be put into the form $ax + b = 0$, where a and b are constants, and $a \neq 0$.

For example, $2x + 3 = 4$ is a linear equation, because it is equivalent to the equation:

$$2x + -1 = 0.$$

And $2x^2 + 3 = 4$ is not a linear equation.

Example:

Solve for x.

$$4x + 3 = 2x + 9$$

Solution:

Put similar terms on the same side of the equality.

$$4x + 3 - 2x = 2x + 9 - 2x$$

$$2x + 3 = 9$$

$$2x = 6$$

$$x = 3$$

Important note: On a multiple choice test, it may sometimes be adequate to check the answers offered.

In order to check the answer "$x = 3$" in the example above, substitute 3 for x in the original equation.

$$4(3) + 3 = 2(3) + 9$$

$$15 = 15 \text{ (True)}$$

If the equation appears in fraction form, it may help to cross-multiply both sides by the denominators.

Example:

Solve for x.

$$\frac{3x + 4}{3} = \frac{7x + 2}{5}$$

Solution:

$$(3x + 4)(5) = (7x + 2)(3)$$

$$15x + 20 = 21x + 6$$

$$14 = 6x$$

$$x = \frac{14}{6} = \frac{7}{3}$$

Example:

Solve for x.

$$-4x + 3 < 5$$

Solution:

Subtract three from both sides.

$$-4x < 2$$

Divide both sides by −4. When both sides of an inequality are multiplied or divided by a negative number, the direction of the inequality changes. (If you forget this fact, you can rediscover it quickly by experimenting. Start with 2 < 4, and see what happens if you divide both sides by −2.)

$$\frac{-4x}{-4} > \frac{2}{-4}$$

$$x > \frac{1}{2}$$

Factoring Expressions and Functions

Example:

Remove all common factors from each term.

$$3x^4 + 6x^2y$$

Solution:

$$3x^4 + 6x^2y = 3x^2 (x^2 + 2y)$$

Example:

Multiply: $(2x + 3)(3x + 4)$

Solution:

$$(2x + 3)(3x + 4) = 6x^2 + 9x + 8x + 12 = 6x^2 + 17x + 12$$

Example:

Factor: $6x^2 + 17x + 12$

Partial Solution:

To get $6x^2$ for the first term, try

$$(6x + \underline{\quad})(x + \underline{\quad}) \text{ and}$$

$$(2x + \underline{3})(3x + \underline{4})$$

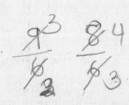

$$2x^2 + 8x + 9x + 12$$

In each case, the product of the numbers in the blanks would have to be the constant term, 12, in the original problem. Eventually, the solution, $(2x + 3)(3x + 4)$, can be found by trial and error.

Factoring formulas:

$$a(c + d) = ac + ad$$

$$(a + b)(a - b) = a^2 - b^2$$

$$(a + b)(a + b) = (a + b)^2 = a^2 + 2ab + b^2$$

$$(a - b)(a - b) = (a - b)^2 = a^2 - 2ab + b^2$$

$$(x + a)(x + b) = x^2 + (ad + bc)x + ab$$

$$(ax + b)(cx + d) = acx^2 + (ad + bc)x + bd$$

$$(a + b)(c + d) = ac + bc + ad + bd$$

$$(a + b)(a + b)(a + b) = (a + b)^3 = a^3 + 3a^2b + 3ab^2 + b^3$$

$$(a - b)(a - b)(a - b) = (a - b)^3 = a^3 - 3a^2b + 3ab^2 - b^3$$

$$(a - b)(a^2 + ab + b^2) = a^3 - b^3$$

$$(a + b)(a^2 - ab + b^2) = a^3 + b^3$$

$$(a + b + c)^2 = a^2 + b^2 + c^2 + 2ab + 2ac + 2bc$$

$$(a - b)(a^3 + a^2b + ab^2 + b^3) = a^4 - b^4$$

$$(a - b)(a^4 + a^3b + a^2b^2 + ab^3 + b^4) = a^5 - b^5$$

$$(a - b)(a^5 - a^4b + a^3b^2 + a^2b^3 + ab^4 + b^5) = a^6 - b^6$$

In general

$$(a - b)(a^{n-1} + a^{n-2}b + a^{n-3}b^2 + \ldots + ab^{n-2} + b^{n-1}) = a^n - b^n$$

where n is any positive integer (1, 2, 3, 4, ...), and

$$(a + b)(a^{n-1} - a^{n-2}b + a^{n-3}b^2 - \ldots - ab^{n-2} + b^{n-1}) = a^n + b^n$$

where n is any positive integer (1, 3, 5 7, ...).

Completing the Square

Definition:

A **quadratic equation** in one variable is an equation that can be put in the form $ax^2 + bx + c = 0$, where a, b, and c are constants, and $a \neq 0$.

Example:

If $(x - 3)^2 = 16$, then $(x - 3) = 4$ or $(x - 3) = -4$; so x is 7 or -1.

If a quadratic equation can't be solved by factoring, we may proceed by completing the square. That is, we may change the problem so it is similar to the example above.

Example:

Solve for x by completing the square: $x^2 - 6x - 6 = 0$.

Solution:

Move the constant to the right: $x^2 - 6x = 6$.

Square one-half the coefficient of x, and add it to both sides:

$$x^2 - 6x + (-3)^2 = 6 + (-3)^2$$

$$x^2 - 6x + 9 = 15$$

Factor the left side into a square: $(x - 3)^2 = 15$

Continue as in the previous example: $x - 3 = \pm\sqrt{15}$

$$x = 3 \pm \sqrt{15}$$

Example:

Solve for x by completing the square: $2x^2 + 3x = 4$

Solution:

Divide both sides by the coefficient x^2: $x^2 + \left(\dfrac{3}{2}\right)x = 2$

Proceed as in the previous example: $x^2 + \left(\dfrac{3}{2}\right)x + \dfrac{9}{16} = 2 + \dfrac{9}{16}$

$$\left(x + \dfrac{3}{4}\right)^2 = \dfrac{41}{16}$$

$$x = -\dfrac{3}{4} \pm \dfrac{\sqrt{41}}{4}$$

Quadratic Formula, Properties of Roots

If we complete the square in the quadratic equation:

$$ax^2 + bx + c = 0$$

we find

$$x = \dfrac{-b \pm \sqrt{b^2 - 4ac}}{2a}$$

Every quadratic equation can be solved using the quadratic formula, but if factoring works, it is usually easier.

The expression "$b^2 - 4ac$" under the square root symbol is called the discriminant of the quadratic equation. If the discriminant is zero, then both solution (or roots) are the same.

If the discriminant is negative, then the roots are not real numbers; they are complex numbers, because the square root of a negative number is imaginary (that is, it needs to be written in terms of i).

If the discriminant is positive, then there are two different real solutions.

Systems of Equations

There are several ways to solve the following system of linear equations.

$$2x + 4y = 11$$

$$-5x + 3y = 5$$

These equations are called linear, because their graphs are straight lines.

First method: If necessary, multiply the equations by numbers that will make the coefficients of one variable in the resulting equations numerically equal. Then add or subtract to eliminate that variable.

$$5(2x + 4y) = 5(11)$$

$$2(-5x + 3y) = 2(5)$$

$$10x + 20y = 55$$
$$\underline{-10x + 6y = 10}$$
$$26y = 65$$

$$y = \frac{65}{26} = \frac{5}{2}$$

Now substitute $\dfrac{5}{2}$ for y in one of the original equations and solve for x.

$$2x + 4\left(\frac{5}{2}\right) = 11$$

$$2x + 10 = 11$$

$$2x = 1$$

$$x = \frac{1}{2}$$

Second method: Use one equation to express one variable in terms of the other variable. Then substitute the expression into the other equation.

$$2x + 4y = 11$$

$$2x = -4y + 11$$

$$x = \frac{-4y + 11}{2}$$

Substitute for x in the equation $-5x + 3y = 5$.

$$(-5)\left(\frac{-4y + 11}{2}\right) + 3y = 5$$

Eventually we find $y = \frac{5}{2}$, as before.

Substituting $\frac{5}{2}$ for y in the first equation, we can find $x = \frac{1}{2}$.

Third method: We may find approximate solutions for x and y by graphing the equations and estimating the x and y coordinates of the point where graphs cross.

Definition:

An **inconsistent system** of linear equations is a system that has no solution.

For example, the following system is inconsistent.

$$2x + 3y = 4$$

$$4x + 6y = 7$$

We might try to solve this system by multiplying both sides of the first equation by two and subtracting; we would obtain a contradiction.

$$4x + 6y = 8$$
$$\underline{4x + 6y = 7}$$
$$0 = 1$$

If both equations were true, then zero would equal one, so we conclude the two equations could not both be true for any values of x and y.

The graphs of these two equations would be parallel lines.

Definition:

A dependent system of linear equations is a system that has an infinite number of solutions.

For example, the following system is dependent.

$$2x + 3y = 4$$

$$4x + 6y = 8$$

We might try to solve this system by the same method as above.

$$4x + 6y = 8$$
$$\underline{4x + 6y = 8}$$
$$0 = 0$$

Any pair of numbers that is a solution for the first equation is a solution for the second.

The graphs of these two equations are the same line.

EQUATIONS OF HIGHER DEGREES

Cubics and Quartics

Definition:

A **cubic equation** is an equation that can be written in the form

$$ax^3 + bx^2 + cx + d = 0,$$

where a, b, c, and d are constants and a is not zero.

Definition:

A **quartic equation** is an equation that can be written in the form

$$ax^4 + bx^3 + cx^2 + dx + e = 0,$$

where a, b, c, d, and e are constants and a is not zero.

Just as there is a quadratic formula that gives all solutions of any quadratic equation, there are formulas for the solutions of these equations.

But the formulas are complicated, and most mathematicians don't memorize them. So it is reasonable to expect questions on tests to be solvable by other methods.

The first method is factoring.

Example:

Solve for x: $x^4 - x = 0$

Solution:

Factoring, we get

$$x(x^3 - 1) = 0$$

Factoring again by the formula listed in the polynomial review, we get

$$x(x - 1)(x^2 + x + 1) = 0$$

Thus, if any of these factors are zero, the equation is true.

$$x = 0, \text{ or } x - 1 = 0 \text{ or } x^2 + x + 1 = 0$$

The first two equations indicate 0 and 1 are solutions. We can solve the last equation with the quadratic formula to find:

$$x = 0, \text{ or } x = 1, \text{ or}$$

$$x = \frac{-1 + \sqrt{3}i}{2} \text{ or}$$

$$x = \frac{-1 + \sqrt{3}i}{2}$$

The second method is graphing.

We could find approximations of the real solutions to the equation above by graphing

$$y = x^4 - x$$

and guessing the x values for which the graph crosses the x-axis.

Factorial Notation

Definition:

If n is a positive integer, then

$$n! = n(n - 1)(n - 2)...1$$
$$0! = 1$$

Example:

$$4! = 4(3)(2)(1) = 24$$

Binomial Theorem/Expansion

Definition:

$$\binom{n}{k} = \frac{n!}{(n-k)!\,k!}$$

$\binom{n}{k}$ is also written as $n^C k$.

The following equation is the binomial theorem or binomial expansion.

$$(x+y)^n = \sum_{k=0}^{n} \binom{n}{k} x^{n-k} y^k$$

$$= \binom{n}{0} x^n + \binom{n}{1} x^{n-1} y + \binom{n}{2} x^{n-2} y^2 +$$

$$\ldots + \binom{n}{k} x^{n-k} y^k + \binom{n}{n} y^n$$

Example:

Find the expansion of $(a - 2x)^7$.

Solution:

Use the binomial formula:

$$(u+v)^n = u^n + nu^{n-1}v + \frac{n(n-1)}{2} u^{n-2}v^2$$

$$+ \frac{n(n-1)(n-2)}{2 \times 3} u^{n-3}v^3 + \ldots + v^n$$

and substitute a for u and $(-2x)$ for v and 7 for n to obtain:

$$(a-2x)^7 = \left[a + (-2x) \right]^7$$

$$= a^7 + 7a^6(-2x) + \frac{7 \times 6}{2} a^5 (-2x)^2 + \frac{7 \times 6 \times 5}{2 \times 3} a^4 (-2x)^3$$

$$+ \frac{7 \times 6 \times 5 \times 4}{2 \times 3 \times 4} a^3 (-2x)^4 + \frac{7 \times 6 \times 5 \times 4 \times 3}{2 \times 3 \times 4 \times 5} a^2 (-2x)^5$$

$$+ \frac{7 \times 6 \times 5 \times 4 \times 3 \times 2}{2 \times 3 \times 4 \times 5 \times 6} a^1 (-2x)^6 + \frac{7 \times 6 \times 5 \times 4 \times 3 \times 2 \times 1}{2 \times 3 \times 4 \times 5 \times 6 \times 7} a^0 (-2x)^7$$

$$(a-2x)^7 = a^7 - 14a^6x + 84a^5x^2 - 280a^4x^3 + 560a^3x^4 - 672a^2x^5 + 448ax^6 - 128x^7.$$

Pascal's Triangle

The coefficients of $(a + b)^0$, $(a + b)^1$, $(a + b)^2$, ..., $(a + b)^n$, can be obtained from Pascal's Triangle.

$(a + b)^0$									1									
$(a + b)^1$								1		1								
$(a + b)^2$							1		2		1							
$(a + b)^3$						1		3		3		1						
$(a + b)^4$					1		4		6		4		1					
$(a + b)^5$				1		5		10		10		5		1				
$(a + b)^6$			1		6		15		20		15		6		1			
$(a + b)^7$		1		7		21		35		35		21		7		1		
$(a + b)^8$	1		8		28		56		70		56		28		8		1	
$(a + b)^9$	1	9		36		84		126		126		84		36		9		1

Each number in the triangle is the sum of the two numbers above it, or one if it is on the edge.

PLANE GEOMETRY

Areas

Area (A) of a:

square $A = s^2$; where s = side

rectangle $A = lw$; where l = length, w = width

parallelogram $A = bh$; where b = base, h = height

triangle $A = \dfrac{1}{2}bh$; where b = base, h = height

circle $A = \pi r^2$; where π = 3.14, r = radius

Perimeters

Perimeter (P) of a:

square $P = 4s$; where s = side

rectangle $P = 2l + 2w$; where l = length, w = width

triangle $P = a + b + c$; where a, b, and c are the sides

circumference (C) of a circle $C = \pi d$, where π = 3.14, d = diameter

Lines and Angles

Definition:

If A and B are two points on a line, then the line segment $\overline{AB}$ is the set of points on that line between A and B, including A and B. A and B are called the endpoints of $\overline{AB}$.

Definition:

If A is a point on a line, the set of all points on the line on one side of A, together with the point A, is a ray. The endpoint of the ray is A.

Definition:

An **angle** is the union of two rays having the same endpoint.

Example:

The angle shown below may be referred to as $\angle A$, $\angle x$, $\angle CAB$, or $\angle BAC$.

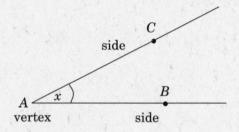

Definition:

Vertical angles are two angles with a common vertex and with sides that are two pairs of opposite rays. (That is, the union of the two pairs of sides is two lines.)

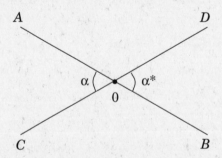

(α and α^* are vertical angles.)

A right angle has a measure of 90°.

An acute angle is an angle whose measure is larger than 0° and smaller than 90°.

An obtuse angle has a measure larger than 90° and less than 180°.

A straight angle has a measure of 180°. The rays of a straight angle lie on a line.

Complementary angles are two angles, the sum of whose measures is 90°.

Supplementary angles are two angles, the sum of whose measure is 180°.

Polygons

A regular polygon has all sides of equal measure and all interior angles of equal measure. The following polygons are regular:

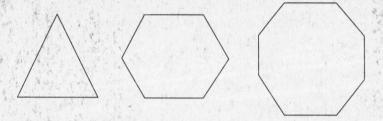

The following polygons are not regular:

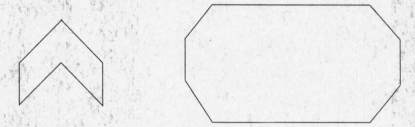

Definition:

An **apothem** of a regular polygon is a line from the center of the polygon to a side of the polygon, perpendicular to the side.

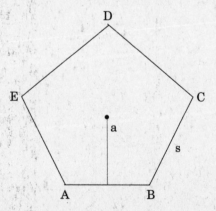

Figure *ABCDE* is a regular polygon with five sides of length *s* and apothem of length a. The area is

$$A = \frac{5as}{2}$$

The area of a regular polygon of n sides, each side of length s, and with apothem of length a, is equal to the product of one-half the polygon's apothem and its perimeter:

$$\text{Area} = \frac{1}{2}ans$$

(The perimeter is ns.)

The measure of each interior angle of a regular polygon of n sides is:

$$\frac{n-2}{n}180°$$

SOLID GEOMETRY

Cubes, Cylinders

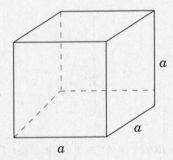

The volume of a cube with edge a is

$$V = a^3.$$

The surface of a cube with edge a is

$$A = 6a^2.$$

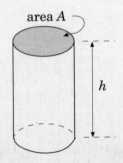

The volume of a right circular cylinder with radius r and height h is

$$V = \pi r^2 h .$$

The surface of a right circular cylinder with radius r and height h is

$$A = 2\pi r^2 + 2\pi rh .$$

Intersecting Planes

If two different planes intersect, they intersect in a straight line.

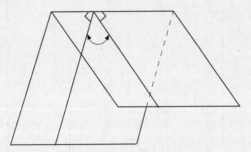

The angle between two planes is the angle between two rays on the two planes, each of which is perpendicular to the line of intersection of the planes.

Volume and Surface Area

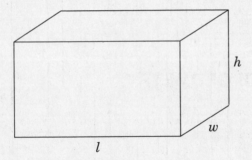

Rectangular solid

The volume of a rectangular solid with length l, width w, and height h is

$$V = lwh.$$

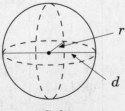

Sphere

The volume of a sphere with radius r is
$$V = \frac{4}{3}\pi r^3.$$
The surface area of a sphere with radius r is
$$A = 4\pi r^2.$$

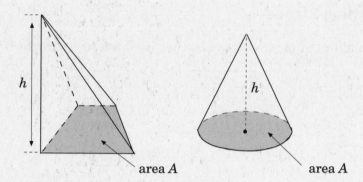

Pyramid   Cone

The volume of a pyramid or cone with base A of area and height h is
$$V = \frac{1}{3}Ah .$$

If the base of the cone is a circle with radius r, then
$$A = \pi r^2,$$

so
$$V = \frac{1}{3}\pi r^2 h.$$

COORDINATE GEOMETRY

Distance

The distance from (x_1, y_1) to (x_2, y_2) is
$$d = \sqrt{(x_2 - x_1)^2 + (y_2 - y_1)^2} .$$

If you forget the formula, it can be found using the Pythagorean theorem, which says that in a right triangle with hypotenuse c and legs a and b,
$$c^2 = a^2 + b^2$$

If you don't know the distance formula and you do know the Pythagorean theorem, you could practice drawing the figure above and rediscovering the distance formula.

Slope

The slope of the line from (x_1, y_1) to (x_2, y_2) is

$$m = \frac{y_2 - y_1}{x_2 - x_1}.$$

The slope may be found by dividing the rise by the run.

Properties of Straight Lines

If m and b are real numbers, then the graph of the equation

$$y = mx + b$$

has slope $= m$ and y-intercept $= b$.

The equation of the line from (x_1, y_1) to (x_2, y_2) is

$$y - y_1 = m(x - x_1),$$

where m is the slope given in the above section.

Graphing Inequalities

Example:

Graph the values of x for which $x^2 - 1 < 0$

Solution:

Since there is only one variable, we may graph the solution on a number line. If we let $y = x^2 - 1$, then we may graph y to find what values of x make $y < 0$.

x	$x^2 - 1$	y
-2	$(-2)^2 - 1$	3
-1	$(-1)^2 - 1$	0
0	$0^2 - 1$	-1
1	$1^2 - 1$	0
2	$2^2 - 1$	3

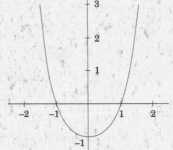

Graph of $y = x^2 - 1$

The graph indicates $y < 0$ if x is between -1 and 1.

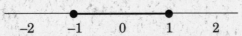

Example:

Graph $y > x^2 - 1$

Any point on the curve in the previous example represents values of x and y for which $y = x^2 - 1$. If we look at any distance directly above such a point, we find a point where $x^2 - 1$ is the same as before (because the x-coordinate hasn't changed) but the y-coordinate is larger than the previous y-coordinate.

So for any point above the graph of $y = x^2 - 1$, we have $y > x^2 - 1$.

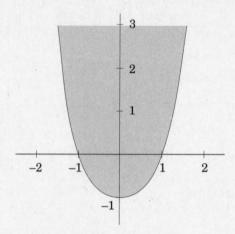

Conic Sections–Parabola, Hyperbola, Ellipse, Circle

In mathematics, the word "cone" refers to the union of two infinitely long pieces, each of which might be called a "cone" in common language.

The intersection of a cone and a plane is called a conic section (unless the intersection includes the one point where the two main sections meet).

CIRCLE: If the cone pictured above is cut by a horizontal plane, the intersection of the plane and the cone is a circle.

The equation of a circle with center (h, k) and radius r is

$$(x - h)^2 + (y - k)^2 = r^2 .$$

ELLIPSE: If the cone pictured above is cut by a plane that is not quite horizontal, the intersection of the plane and the cone is an ellipse.

If $a^2 \neq b^2$, then the graph of the following equation is an ellipse with center at the origin.

$$\frac{x^2}{a^2} + \frac{y^2}{b^2} = 1$$

The x-intercepts of the ellipse are $-a$ and a. The y-intercepts are $-b$ and b. If $a^2 > b^2$, then the ellipse has foci at points $-c$ and c on the x-axis, where

$$c = \sqrt{a^2 - b^2} \ .$$

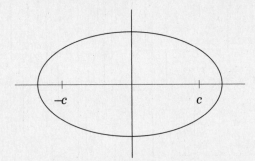

Ellipse with foci at $-c$ and c

The sum of the distances to the two foci is the same for any two points on the ellipse.

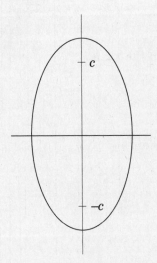

Ellipse with foci at $-c$ and c

If $b^2 > a^2$, then the ellipse has foci at points $-c$ and c on the y-axis, where

$$c = b^2 - a^2 \ .$$

If we replace x and y by $x - h$ and $y - k$ respectively in the equation of the ellipse, then the graph will be an ellipse congruent to the original, with center at (h, k) instead of at the origin.

$$\frac{(x-h)^2}{a^2} + \frac{(y-k)^2}{b^2} = 1$$

PARABOLA: If the plane intersecting the cone is tilted a little more, so that it is parallel to a straight line on one side of the cone, the inter-section of the cone and the plane is called a parabola.

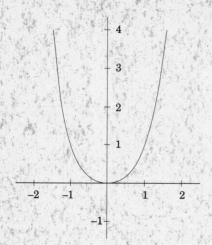

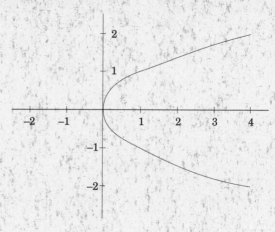

Graph of $y = x^2$.
Parabola with y-axis
as line of symmetry.

Graph of $x = y^2$.
Parabola with x-axis
as line of symmetry.

If a is a constant, then the graph of

$$y = ax^2$$

is a parabola through the origin, with the y-axis as a line of symmetry, and the graph of

$$x = ay^2$$

is a parabola through the origin, with the x-axis as a line of symmetry.

As before, we will get congruent parabolas through (h, k) if we replace x and y by $(x - h)$ and $(y - k)$ respectively in the equations above.

$$y - k = a(x - h)^2$$

$$x - h = a(y - k)^2$$

HYPERBOLA: If the plane cutting the cone is tilted enough that it hits both the top and bottom sections of the cone, then the intersection of the plane and the cone is called a hyperbola.

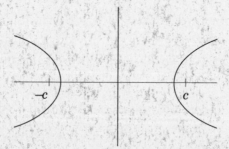

Hyperbola with foci at $-c$ and c

The equation of a hyperbola with foci at $-c$ and c on the x-axis is

$$\frac{x^2}{a^2} - \frac{y^2}{c^2 - a^2} = 1$$

The difference of the distances to the foci is the same for any two points on the hyperbola.

The x-intercepts of the hyperbola are at $-a$ and a.

If we interchange x and y, the graph is a hyperbola with y-intercepts at $-a$ and a and foci at $-c$ and c on y-axis.

$$\frac{y^2}{a^2} - \frac{x^2}{c^2 - a^2} = 1$$

Again, we may shift the graph to have center (h, k) instead of center at the origin, by replacing x and y by $x - h$ and $y - k$ respectively.

TRIGONOMETRY

Angles and Trigonometric Functions

Given a right triangle $\triangle ABC$ as shown in the figure below:

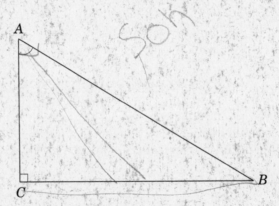

Definition 1:

$$\sin \angle A = \frac{BC}{AB}$$

$$= \frac{\text{measure of side opposite } \angle A}{\text{measure of hypotenuse}}$$

Definition 2:

$$\cos \angle A = \frac{AC}{AB}$$

$$= \frac{\text{measure of side adjacent to } \angle A}{\text{measure of hypotenuse}}$$

Definition 3:

$$\tan \angle A = \frac{BC}{AC}$$

$$= \frac{\text{measure of side opposite } \angle A}{\text{measure of side adjacent to } \angle A}$$

Definition 4:

$$\cot \angle A = \frac{AC}{BC}$$

$$= \frac{\text{measure of side adjacent to } \angle A}{\text{measure of side opposite } \angle A}$$

$$\sec \angle A = \frac{AB}{AC}$$

$$= \frac{\text{measure of hypotenuse}}{\text{measure of side adjacent to } \angle A}$$

$$\csc \angle A = \frac{AB}{BC}$$

$$= \frac{\text{measure of hypotenuse}}{\text{measure of side opposite } \angle A}$$

The following table gives the values of sine, cosine, tangent, and cotangent for some special angles. The angles are given in radians and in degrees.

α	$\sin \alpha$	$\cos \alpha$	$\tan \alpha$	$\cot \alpha$
$0°$	0	1	0	∞
$\dfrac{\pi}{6} = 30°$	$\dfrac{1}{2}$	$\dfrac{\sqrt{3}}{2}$	$\dfrac{1}{\sqrt{3}}$	$\sqrt{3}$
$\dfrac{\pi}{4} = 45°$	$\dfrac{1}{\sqrt{2}}$	$\dfrac{1}{\sqrt{2}}$	1	1
$\dfrac{\pi}{3} = 60°$	$\dfrac{\sqrt{3}}{2}$	$\dfrac{1}{2}$	$\sqrt{3}$	$\dfrac{1}{\sqrt{3}}$
$\dfrac{\pi}{2} = 90°$	1	0	∞	0

A circle with center located at the origin of the rectangular coordinate axes and radius equal to one unit length is called a unit circle.

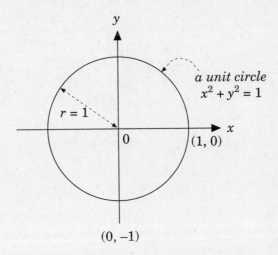

An angle whose vertex is at the origin of a rectangular coordinate system and whose initial side coincides with the positive x-axis is said to be in standard position with respect to the coordinate system.

An angle in standard position with respect to a cartesian coordinate system whose terminal side lies in the first (or second or third or fourth) quadrant is called a first (or second or third or fourth) quadrant angle.

A quadrant angle is an angle in standard position whose terminal side lies on one of the axes of a cartesian coordinate system.

If θ is a non-quadrantal angle in standard position and $P(x, y)$ is any point, distinct from the origin, on the terminal side of θ, then the six trigonometric functions of θ are defined in terms of the abscissa (x-coordinate), ordinate (y-coordinate), and distance $\overline{OP}$ as follows:

$$\text{sine } \theta = \sin\theta = \frac{\text{ordinate}}{\text{distance}} = \frac{y}{r}$$

$$\text{cosine } \theta = \cos\theta = \frac{\text{abscissa}}{\text{distance}} = \frac{x}{r}$$

$$\text{tangent } \theta = \tan\theta = \frac{\text{ordinate}}{\text{abscissa}} = \frac{y}{x}$$

$$\text{cotangent } \theta = \cot\theta = \frac{\text{abscissa}}{\text{ordinate}} = \frac{x}{y}$$

$$\text{secant } \theta = \sec\theta = \frac{\text{distance}}{\text{abscissa}} = \frac{r}{x}$$

$$\text{cosecant } \theta = \csc \theta = \frac{\text{distance}}{\text{ordinate}} = \frac{r}{y}$$

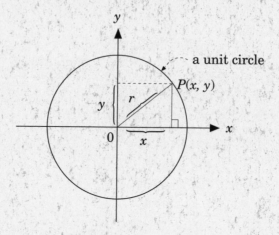

The value of trigonometric functions of quadrantal angles are given in the table below.

θ	sinθ	cosθ	tanθ	cotθ	secθ	cscθ
0°	0	1	0	±∞	1	±∞
90°	1	0	±∞	0	±∞	1
180°	0	−1	0	±∞	−1	±∞
270°	−1	0	±∞	0	±∞	−1

Basic Identities

$$\sin^2 \alpha + \cos^2 \alpha = 1$$

$$\tan \alpha = \frac{\sin \alpha}{\cos \alpha}$$

$$\cot\alpha = \frac{\cos\alpha}{\sin\alpha} = \frac{1}{\tan\alpha}$$

$$\csc\alpha = \frac{1}{\sin\alpha}$$

$$\sec\alpha = \frac{1}{\cos\alpha}$$

$$1 + \tan^2\alpha = \sec^2\alpha$$

$$1 + \cot^2\alpha = \csc^2\alpha$$

One can find all the trigonometric functions of an acute angle when the value of any one of them is known.

For example, given α is an acute angle and $\csc\alpha = 2$, then

$$\sin\alpha = \frac{1}{\csc\alpha} = \frac{1}{2}$$

$$\cos^2\alpha + \sin^2\alpha = 1, \cos\alpha = \sqrt{1 - \sin^2\alpha}$$

$$= \sqrt{1 - \left(\frac{1}{2}\right)^2}$$

$$= \sqrt{1 - \frac{1}{4}}$$

$$= \frac{\sqrt{3}}{2}$$

$$\tan\alpha = \frac{\sin\alpha}{\cos\alpha} = \frac{\frac{1}{2}}{\frac{\sqrt{3}}{2}} = \frac{1}{\sqrt{3}} = \frac{\sqrt{3}}{3}$$

$$\cot\alpha = \frac{1}{\tan\alpha} = \sqrt{3}$$

$$\sec\alpha = \frac{1}{\cos\alpha} = \frac{1}{\frac{\sqrt{3}}{2}} = \frac{2}{\sqrt{3}} = \frac{2\sqrt{3}}{3}$$

For a given angle θ in standard position, the related angle θ is the unique acute angle that the terminal side of θ makes with the *x*-axis.

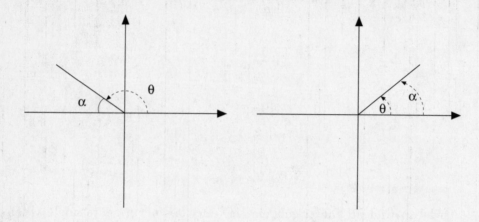

∠α is the related angle of ∠θ   ∠α is the related angle of ∠θ

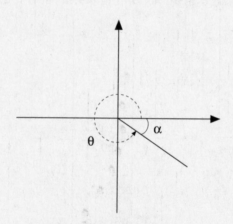

∠α is the related angle of ∠θ

Let θ be an angle in standard position and ϕ be the related angle of θ.

i)   If θ is a first quadrant angle, then

   a)   sin θ = sin ϕ

   b)   cos θ = cos ϕ

   c)   tan θ = tan ϕ

   d)   cot θ = cot ϕ

   e)   sec θ = sec ϕ

   f)   csc θ = csc ϕ

ii) If θ is a second quadrant angle, then

   a)   sin θ = sin ϕ

   b)   cos θ = −cos ϕ

c) $\tan \theta = -\tan \phi$

d) $\cot \theta = -\cot \phi$

e) $\sec \theta = -\sec \phi$

f) $\csc \theta = \csc \phi$

iii) If θ is a third quadrant angle, then

   a) $\sin \theta = -\sin \phi$

   b) $\cos \theta = -\cos \phi$

   c) $\tan \theta = \tan \phi$

   d) $\cot \theta = \cot \phi$

   e) $\sec \theta = -\sec \phi$

   f) $\csc \theta = -\csc \phi$

iv) If θ is a fourth quadrant angle, then

   a) $\sin \theta = -\sin \phi$

   b) $\cos \theta = \cos \phi$

   c) $\tan \theta = -\tan \phi$

   d) $\cot \theta = -\cot \phi$

   e) $\sec \theta = \sec \phi$

   f) $\csc \theta = -\csc \phi$

	sin	cos	tan	cot	sec	csc
$-\alpha$	$-\sin \alpha$	$+\cos \alpha$	$-\tan \alpha$	$-\cot \alpha$	$+\sec \alpha$	$-\csc \alpha$
$90° + \alpha$	$+\cos \alpha$	$-\sin \alpha$	$-\cot \alpha$	$-\tan \alpha$	$-\csc \alpha$	$+\sec \alpha$
$90° - \alpha$	$+\cos \alpha$	$+\sin \alpha$	$+\cot \alpha$	$+\tan \alpha$	$+\csc \alpha$	$+\sec \alpha$
$180° + \alpha$	$-\sin \alpha$	$-\cos \alpha$	$+\tan \alpha$	$+\cot \alpha$	$-\sec \alpha$	$-\csc \alpha$
$180° - \alpha$	$+\sin \alpha$	$-\cos \alpha$	$-\tan \alpha$	$-\cot \alpha$	$-\sec \alpha$	$+\csc \alpha$
$270° + \alpha$	$-\cos \alpha$	$+\sin \alpha$	$-\cot \alpha$	$-\tan \alpha$	$+\csc \alpha$	$-\sec \alpha$
$270° - \alpha$	$-\cos \alpha$	$-\sin \alpha$	$+\cot \alpha$	$+\tan \alpha$	$-\csc \alpha$	$-\sec \alpha$
$360° + \alpha$	$+\sin \alpha$	$+\cos \alpha$	$+\tan \alpha$	$+\cot \alpha$	$+\sec \alpha$	$+\csc \alpha$
$360° - \alpha$	$-\sin \alpha$	$+\cos \alpha$	$-\tan \alpha$	$-\cot \alpha$	$+\sec \alpha$	$-\csc \alpha$

Addition and Subtraction Formulas

$$\sin(A \pm B) = \sin A \cos B \pm \cos A \sin B$$

$$\cos(A \pm B) = \cos A \cos B \pm \sin A \sin B$$

$$\tan(A \pm B) = \frac{\tan A \pm \tan B}{1 \pm \tan A \tan B}$$

$$\cot(A \pm B) = \frac{\cot A \cot B \pm 1}{\cot B \pm \cot A}$$

Double-angle Formulas

$$\sin 2A = 2 \sin A \cos A$$

$$\cos 2A = 2 \cos^2 A - 1$$

$$= 1 - 2 \sin^2 A$$

$$= \cos^2 A - \sin^2 A$$

$$\tan 2A = \frac{2 \tan A}{1 - \tan^2 A}$$

Half-angle Formulas

$$\sin \frac{A}{2} = \pm \frac{\sqrt{1 - \cos A}}{2}$$

$$\cos \frac{A}{2} = \pm \frac{\sqrt{1 + \cos A}}{2}$$

$$\tan \frac{A}{2} = \pm \frac{\sqrt{1 - \cos A}}{1 + \cos A}$$

$$= \frac{1 - \cos A}{\sin A}$$

$$= \frac{\sin A}{1 + \cos A}$$

$$\cot \frac{A}{2} = \pm \frac{\sqrt{1 + \cos A}}{1 - \cos A} = \frac{1 + \cos A}{\sin A} = \frac{\sin A}{1 - \cos A}$$

Sum and Difference Formulas

$$\sin\alpha + \sin\beta = 2\sin\left(\frac{\alpha+\beta}{2}\right)\cos\left(\frac{\alpha-\beta}{2}\right)$$

$$\sin\alpha - \sin\beta = 2\cos\left(\frac{\alpha+\beta}{2}\right)\sin\left(\frac{\alpha-\beta}{2}\right)$$

$$\cos\alpha + \cos\beta = 2\cos\left(\frac{\alpha+\beta}{2}\right)\cos\left(\frac{\alpha-\beta}{2}\right)$$

$$\cos\alpha - \cos\beta = -2\sin\left(\frac{\alpha+\beta}{2}\right)\sin\left(\frac{\alpha-\beta}{2}\right)$$

$$\tan\alpha + \tan\beta = \frac{\sin(\alpha+\beta)}{\cos\alpha\cos\beta}$$

$$\tan\alpha \times \tan\beta = \frac{\sin(\alpha-\beta)}{\cos\alpha\cos\beta}$$

Product Formulas of Sines and Cosines

$$\sin A \sin B = \frac{1}{2}\left[\cos(A-B) - \cos(A+B)\right]$$

$$\cos A \cos B = \frac{1}{2}\left[\cos(A+B) + \cos(A-B)\right]$$

$$\sin A \cos B = \frac{1}{2}\left[\sin(A+B) + \sin(A-B)\right]$$

$$\cos A \sin B = \frac{1}{2}\left[\sin(A+B) - \sin(A-B)\right]$$

Solving Right Triangles

If we know the measures (lengths) of two sides of a right triangle, then we can find the measures of the other side and all the angles of the triangle.

Example:

Find the measures of the angles and sides in the following triangle, given $\overline{AB} = 6$, $\overline{BC} = 3$ and $\angle C = 90$.

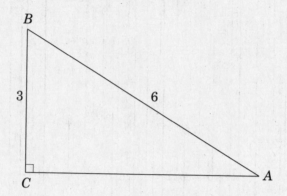

Solution:

$$\sin \angle A = \frac{3}{6} = \frac{1}{2}$$

From a table of trigonometric functions or a calculator, we find

$$\angle A = 30°.$$

The definition of the cotangent indicates that for this triangle,

$$\text{cotangent } \angle A = \frac{AC}{6}$$

so $\overline{AC} = 6$ cotangent 30°.

From a table, we find cotangent $30° = \dfrac{\sqrt{3}}{2}$. Substituting in the equation above, we find:

$$\overline{AC} = 6\left(\frac{\sqrt{3}}{2}\right) = 3\sqrt{3}.$$

Similarly, given the measures of a side and an acute angle of a right triangle, we can find the measures of each of the other parts.

ELEMENTARY FUNCTIONS

Logarithms and Exponentials

An exponential function, f, is a function of the form

$$f(x) = ab^x,$$

where a is a non-zero, and b (the base of the function) is positive.

For example, if

$$f(x) = 10^x,$$

then

$$f(1) = 10^1 = 10, \text{ and}$$
$$f(2) = 10^2 = 100$$

Definition:

$\log_b N$ = the exponent needed on b to produce N.

That is, if $b^x = N$, then $\log_b N = x$.

The base of the logarithm is b.

For example,

$$\log_{10} 100 = 2, \text{ because } 10^2 = 100.$$

Example:

Since $10^2(10^3) = 10^5$, we conclude

$$\log_{10} 10^2(10^3) = \log_{10} 10^2 + \log_{10} 10^3$$

(That is, $5 = 2 + 3$.)

This example could remind you of the first of the following logarithm formulas if you forget it. The other rules follow from similar rules of exponents.

Logarithm Formulas:

$$\log_b MN = \log_b M + \log_b N$$
$$\log_b M/N = \log_b M - \log_b N$$
$$\log_b N^k = k \log_b N$$

There is a constant, e, called the natural base (approximately 2.7), which is used as a base to make exponential functions and logarithmic functions easier for problems in calculus.

Composite Functions

Example:

Find $f(g(2))$ if

$$f(x) = x^2 - 3$$
$$g(x) = 3x + 1$$

Solution:

$$g(2) = 3(2) + 1 = 7$$

Substitute 7 for $g(2)$.

$$f(g(2)) = f(7) = 7^2 - 3 = 46$$

The functions f and g may be pictured as follows:

$$2 \xrightarrow{\quad\quad g \quad\quad} 7$$

The composite function fg may be pictured as follows:

$$2 \xrightarrow{\quad\quad\quad fg \quad\quad\quad} 46$$

The composite function fg is defined by

$$f \times g(x) = f(g(x))$$

Composite functions are useful in related rate problems, and other problems of calculus.

Absolute Value Function

Example:

Graph the equation $y = |x|$

Solution:

x	y
-2	2
-1	1
0	0
1	1
2	2

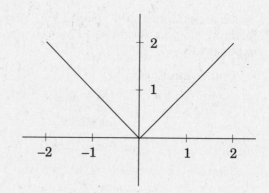

Example:

Graph the equation $y = |x^2 - 1|$

Solution:

Refer to the graph of $y = x^2 - 1$. Replace any point that has a negative y-coordinate with a point directly above it the same distance from the x-axis.

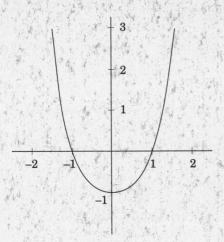

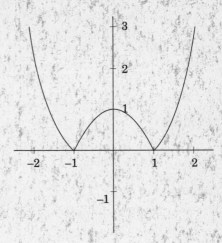

Graph of $y = x^2 - 1$ Graph of $y = |x^2 - 1|$

Explanation: Since $(0, -1)$ is on the graph of $y = x^2 - 1$, when x is 0, $x^2 - 1$ is 1, and so $|x^2 - 1| = 1$. Thus, $(0, 1)$ is on the graph of $y = |x^2 - 1|$.

MISCELLANEOUS TOPICS

Probability

Definition:

An **event** is a set of outcomes of an experiment.

The probability of an event is the fraction of the time the event will occur.

If there are a finite number of equally likely outcomes of an experiment, then the probability of an event, E, is

$$P(E) = \frac{\text{number of outcomes in } E}{\text{total number of possible outcomes}}$$

Example:

A fair die is rolled. What is the probability the result is greater than 4?

Solution:

There are two outcomes greater than four, and there are six possible outcomes all together, (namely 1, 2, 3, 4, 5, and 6); so the probability is:

$$P(\{5,6\}) = \frac{2}{6} = \frac{1}{3}$$

The probability that events A and B will both occur is the probability of AB.

$$P(A \text{ and } B) = P(A \cap B)$$

Example:

A fair die is rolled. What is the probability the result is greater than 4 and the result is even?

Solution:

The set of outcomes that are greater than four and even is $\{6\}$. So the probability is:

$$P(\{6\}) = \frac{1}{6}$$

The probability the event A or the event B will occur is:

$$P(A \text{ or } B) = P(A \cup B)$$

Example:

A fair die is rolled. What is the probability the result is greater than 4 or the result is even?

Solution:

The set of outcomes that are greater than four or even is $\{2,4,5,6\}$. So the probability is:

$$P(\{2,4,5,6\}) = \frac{4}{6} = \frac{2}{3}$$

The conditional probability of event B given event A is the fraction of the times that B occurs among just the times that A occurs.

The conditional probability of B given A is given by the formula:

$$P\left(\frac{B}{A}\right) = \frac{P(B \cap A)}{P(A)}$$

Example:

A fair die is rolled. What is the conditional probability the result is even given the result is greater than 3?

Solution:

The outcomes greater than 3 are $\{4,5,6\}$. Among those outcomes, the outcome is even two-thirds of the time.

$$P(\{2,4,6\}|\{4,5,6\}) = \frac{P(\{4,6\})}{P(\{4,5,6\})} = \frac{\dfrac{2}{6}}{\dfrac{3}{6}} = \frac{2}{3}$$

Logic

In mathematics, if two statements are connected with "or," then the compound statement is true if either or both of the original statements is true.

Examples:

$2 < 3$ or $5 < 7$ True

$2 < 3$ or $5 < 3$ True

$2 < 1$ or $5 < 7$ True

$2 < 1$ or $5 < 3$ False

This mathematical tradition is sometimes followed in common speech. Suppose people are allowed to attend a movie if they are over 17 or accompanied by their parent, and an eighteen-year-old goes to the theater alone. Then the statement that the person is accompanied by his or her parent is false.

The statement that the person is over 17 or accompanied by a parent is true. This example may help you remember how to handle statements containing the word "or."

If two statements are connected by "and," then the compound statement is true if and only if both statements are true.

Examples:

$2 < 3$ and $5 < 7$ True

$2 < 3$ and $5 < 3$ False

$2 < 1$ and $5 < 7$ False

$2 < 1$ and $5 < 3$ False

DeMorgan's Laws:

The compound statement "p and q" is false if and only if "not p" or "not q" is true.

The compound statement "p or q" is false if and only if "not p" or "not q" is true.

Elementary Number Theory, Counting Problems

Definition:

An integer greater than 1 that has no factors other than 1 and itself is called **prime**.

The prime numbers in the following list are underlined.

2 <u>3</u> 4 <u>5</u> 6 <u>7</u> 8 9 10 <u>11</u> 12 <u>13</u> 14 15 16 <u>17</u> 18 <u>19</u> 20 21 22 <u>23</u> 24 25

Definition:

An integer greater than 1 that is not prime is called **composite**. The numbers in the list above that are not underlined are composite.

Definition:

If a and b have no prime factors in common, then a and b are **relatively prime**.

Example:

Eight and nine are relatively prime, because

$$8 = 2(2)(2), \text{ and}$$

$$9 = 3(3).$$

There are no primes in the first factorization that appear in the second factorization.

The fraction $\dfrac{a}{b}$ is in lowest terms if and only if a and b are relatively prime. So the fraction $\dfrac{8}{9}$ is in lowest terms.

Example:

Mary wants to wear one of two necklaces and one of three bracelets. How many different combinations of jewelry will she consider?

Solution:

We may draw a tree diagram listing all her possible choices. First, she can choose a necklace.

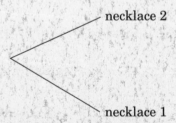

necklace 2

necklace 1

After she has chosen a necklace, there are three ways to choose a bracelet in each case.

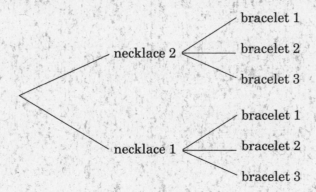

So there are six ways of choosing a necklace and then a bracelet.

Example:

How many ways may a committee of three people be chosen from a group of ten people?

Solution:

The formula for the number of combinations of n things taken k at a time (where the order of the selection doesn't matter) is

$$n^C k = \frac{n!}{(n-k)!\,k!}$$

To find the number of ways to choose three people from a group of ten people, where the order doesn't matter, replace n with ten and k with three in the formula above.

$$10^C 3 = \frac{10!}{(10-3)!\,3!} = \frac{10!}{7!\,3!} = \frac{10(9)(8)(7)(6)(5)(4)(3)(2)(1)}{7(6)(5)(4)(3)(2)(1)} = \frac{10(9)(8)}{3(2)(1)} = 120$$

Example:

How many ways may a president, vice president, and secretary be chosen from a group of ten people?

Solution:

The formula for the number of permutations of n things taken k at a time (where the order of the selection matters) is

$$n^P k = \frac{n!}{(n-k)!}$$

To find the number of ways to choose three people from a group of ten people, where the order matters, replace n with ten and k with three in the formula on the previous page.

$$10^P3 = \frac{10!}{(10-3)!} = \frac{10!}{7!3!} = \frac{10(9)(8)(7)(6)(5)(4)(3)(2)(1)}{7(6)(5)(4)(3)(2)(1)} = 10(9)(8) = 720$$

The order of selection matters when we choose president, vice president, and secretary, because if Mary is president and Jane is vice president, we have a different solution than if Jane is president and Mary is vice president.

The order of selection doesn't matter when we choose a committee, because the committee consisting of Mary, Jane, and Bob is the same as the committee consisting of Jane, Mary, and Bob.

If you forget which formula is used where the order matters, you may remember that there are more solutions where the order matters; so you would want to choose the formula that produced the larger number. That is the formula without $k!$ in the denominator, because the smaller denominator makes a larger fraction.

If you forget the formulas altogether, the permutation formula can be found quickly using a tree diagram.

Sets—Union and Intersection

Definition:

The **union** of the sets A and B is the set of all points that are in A or in B.

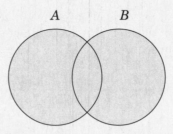

$A \cup B$ is shaded.

Example:

What is the union of the sets {1,3,5} and {1,5,6}?

Solution:

{1,3,4,5,6}

Definition:

The **intersection** of the sets A and B is the set of all points that are in both A and B.

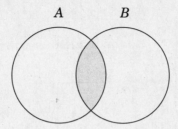

$A \cap B$ is shaded.

Example:

What is the intersection of the sets {1,3,5} and {1,5,6}?

Solution:

{1,5}

THE SAT SUBJECT TEST IN

Math
Level 1

PRACTICE TEST 1

SAT Mathematics Level 1

Practice Test 1

Time: 1 Hour
50 Questions

DIRECTIONS: Choose the best answer for each question and mark the letter of your selection on the corresponding answer sheet.

NOTES:

(1)   Some questions require the use of a calculator. You must decide when the use of your calculator will be helpful.

(2)   Make sure your calculator is in degree mode.

(3)   All figures are drawn to scale and lie in a plane unless otherwise stated.

(4)   The domain of any function f is the set of all real numbers x for which $f(x)$ is a real number, unless other information is provided.

REFERENCE INFORMATION: The following information may be helpful in answering some of the questions.

Volume of a right circular cone with radius r and height h	$V = \dfrac{1}{3}\pi r^2 h$
Lateral area of a right circular cone with circumference c and slant height l	$S = \dfrac{1}{2}cl$
Volume of a sphere with radius r	$V = \dfrac{4}{3}\pi r^3$
Surface area of a sphere with radius r	$S = 4\pi r^2$
Volume of a pyramid with base area B and height h	$V = \dfrac{1}{3}Bh$

1. John works at a gas station and is paid $6/hour. If the federal government takes 24% of his earnings and the state takes 1/4 as much as the federal government does, how much does John take home after a 30 hour week?

    (A) $43.20

    (D) $136.80

    (B) $54.00

    (E) $180.00

    (C) $126.00

2. Given the equation $\dfrac{7x}{3} = (a^4 + 1)^3$, and $a = -1$, solve for x.

    (A) 16

    (D) $\dfrac{20}{3}$

    (B) $\dfrac{24}{7}$

    (E) 0

    (C) 24

3. What three consecutive integers add up to 1,494?

    (A) 488, 489, 490

    (D) 497, 498, 499

    (B) 496, 498, 500

    (E) 490, 498, 506

    (C) $1,494 - x$, $1,494 - y$, $1,494 - z$

4. A cube of styrofoam with side length of 5 feet is given four equally spaced cuts perpendicular to one face and then is rotated 90° degrees and cut in the same way. How many congruent rectangular solids are formed?

    (A) 125

    (D) 16

    (B) 25

    (E) None of the above.

    (C) 64

5. The resulting cut cube from above is rotated 90° perpendicularly and then cut again in the same fashion. How many congruent cubes are formed?

    (A) No change.

    (D) 64.

    (B) 125.

    (E) 16.

    (C) 25.

6. Determine the roots of the following quadratic: $0 = x^2 - 7x + 10$.

    (A) $x = 5$ and $x = 2$ (D) $x = 1$ and $x = -8$

    (B) $x = -5$ and $x = -2$ (E) No real roots.

    (C) $x = -1$ and $x = 8$

7. In the figure, $\overline{AB} = 8$ and $\overline{BC} = 2$. What is the area of region $BCDE$, if $\triangle ABE$ and $\triangle ACD$ are equilateral?

    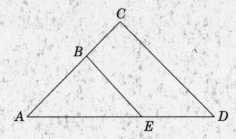

    (A) $\dfrac{\sqrt{3}}{2}$ (D) $9\sqrt{3}$

    (B) 18   (E) $\dfrac{35\sqrt{2}}{2}$

    (C) 50

8. If $f(x) = 7x^2 + 3$ and $g(x) = 2x - 9$, $g(f(2)) =$

    (A) 28.   (D) 19.

    (B) 0.   (E) 53.

    (C) 31.

For Problems 9–11 refer to the grid below

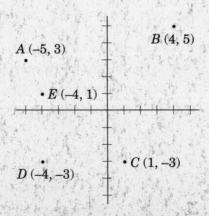

9. Which pair of points has a slope of –1?

   (A) *A, B*   (D) *A, D*

   (B) *B, C*   (E) *B, D*

   (C) *A, C*

10. What is the slope of a line connecting points *B* and *C*?

    (A) –0.375   (D) 2.667

    (B) 0.375   (E) –0.500

    (C) –2.667

11. What is the distance from *A* to *D*?

    (A) 10.820   (D) 1.000

    (B) 6.083   (E) 9.000

    (C) 6.000

12. The solution set to the system: $\begin{cases} 2x + 3y = 6 \\ y - 2 = \dfrac{-2x}{3} \end{cases}$ is

    (A) {0, 2}.   (D) {8, 3}.

    (B) {0, 0}.   (E) infinite.

    (C) $\left\{\dfrac{1}{3}, 5\right\}$.

13. Determine the real roots of the following quadratic: $0 = x^2 + 4x + 6$.

    (A) –0.5858 and –3.4142   (D) 0.75 and 1.25

    (B) 0.5858 and 3.4142   (E) No real roots.

    (C) –0.75 and –1.25

14. In which quadrants does the solution of the system $\begin{cases} y < -x + 3 \\ y < x - 3 \end{cases}$ lie?

    (A) III and IV   (D) I and II

    (B) I, III, and IV   (E) II and III

    (C) II and IV

15. The ratio of the areas of two circles is 25:16. How much longer is the diameter of the larger circle than that of the smaller circle?

(A) $\dfrac{5}{4}$ (D) $\dfrac{25}{4}$

(B) $\dfrac{5}{2}$ (E) 4

(C) 5

16. The greatest area that a rectangle whose perimeter is 52m can have is

(A) 12m^2.   (D) 168m^2.

(B) 169m^2.   (E) 52m^2.

(C) 172m^2.

17. In the figure, which of the following must be true for $\overline{BD} \parallel \overline{AE}$?

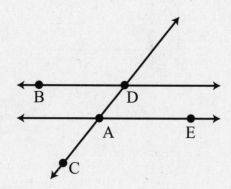

I. $\angle BAD = \angle ADE$

II. $\angle BDA = \angle DAE$

III. $\angle CBD = \angle BDC$

(A) I only   (D) II only

(B) I and II only   (E) III only

(C) II and III only

18. A given sphere has a surface area of $64\pi m^2$. It is then cut in half. The volume occupied by the half sphere is

    (A) $256\pi m^3$.

    (B) $\dfrac{256}{3}\pi m^3$.

    (C) $\dfrac{128}{3}\pi m^3$.

    (D) $\dfrac{512}{3}\pi m^3$.

    (E) $\dfrac{64}{9}\pi m^3$.

19. Find the sum of the interior angles of a nine-sided regular polygon.

    (A) 360°

    (B) 900°

    (C) 1,260°

    (D) 1,440°

    (E) 1,620°

20. Given two circles, the first with a radius of 5, how large is the radius of the second circle if its circumference is twice as large as the first?

    (A) 2.5

    (B) 5

    (C) 7.07

    (D) 10

    (E) 25

21. Of the following relations, the ones that are functions are

    I. $\dfrac{x^2}{81} - \dfrac{y^2}{16} = 3$

    II. $x^2 + \left| \dfrac{\sqrt{y^2}}{3} \right| = 3y$

    III. $y = \sqrt{3}x$

    (A) I

    (B) I and III

    (C) II

    (D) I, II, and III

    (E) II and III

22. Determine the measure of ∠*AEC*.

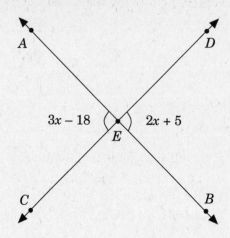

(A) 45°

(B) 90°

(C) 23°

(D) 31.8°

(E) 51°

23. Let $f(x) = 19 + x$, $g(x) = 3x + 1$. $[g(f(-20))]^2 - g(1)$ equals

(A) 1.

(B) −1.

(C) 0.

(D) 3.

(E) −2.

24. Given two circles, the first with a radius of 5, how large is the radius of the second circle if its area is twice as large as the first circle?

(A) 2.50

(B) 5.00

(C) 7.07

(D) 10.00

(E) 25.00

25. When an airplane flies at a speed of 300 miles per hour against the wind, it flies 200 miles in 2 hours. The wind speed is

(A) 200 mph.

(B) 150 mph.

(C) 100 mph.

(D) 250 mph.

(E) None of the above.

26. In the figure, $\sin\angle BCD = \dfrac{1}{2}$, $\overline{BC} = 8$, and $\angle BDC = 90°$. The ratio of the area of $\triangle ABD$ to $\triangle DBC$ is

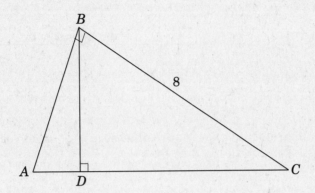

(A) $\dfrac{2}{3}$.

(D) $\dfrac{1}{2}$.

(B) $\dfrac{4}{5}$.

(E) $\dfrac{1}{3}$.

(C) $\dfrac{1}{4}$.

27. Two dice are thrown, one red and one green. The probability that the number on the red exceeds the number showing on the green by exactly two is

(A) $\dfrac{1}{18}$.

(D) $\dfrac{1}{36}$.

(B) $\dfrac{1}{4}$.

(E) $\dfrac{1}{24}$.

(C) $\dfrac{1}{9}$.

28. A circle is defined by $x^2 + y^2 - 6x + 8y = 0$. Find its center.

(A) $(2, 4)$

(D) $(3, -4)$

(B) $(-5, 9)$

(E) $(6, -8)$

(C) $(4, -3)$

29. If a function is defined as $|2 - 5x| < 3$, then the interval which does not contain any solution for x is

(A) $0 < x < 1$.

(B) $0 < x < 2$.

(C) $-\dfrac{1}{25} < x < 0$.

(D) $-\dfrac{3}{5} < x < -\dfrac{1}{2}$.

(E) $-1 < x < 1$.

30. If α and β are acute angles such that $\sec\alpha = \dfrac{17}{15}$ and $\cos\beta = \dfrac{6}{10}$, find $\sin(\alpha + \beta)$.

(A) $\dfrac{84}{85}$

(B) $\dfrac{56}{57}$

(C) $\dfrac{7}{8}$

(D) $\dfrac{37}{38}$

(E) $\dfrac{99}{100}$

31. A hollow cone has a height of 3m, volume of $81\pi m^3$, and is composed of material that weighs 2 kg/m². Find its total mass.

(A) $54\pi\sqrt{10}$ kg

(B) 63π kg

(C) $75\sqrt{3}\,\pi$ kg

(D) $63\sqrt{2}\,\pi$ kg

(E) $81\sqrt{3}\,\pi$ kg

32. If $i = \sqrt{-1}$ and $f(z) = z^2 + 3z + 5$, find $f(2 + i)$.

(A) $6 + 5i$

(B) $14 + 7i$

(C) $10 + 8i$

(D) $3 + 9i$

(E) $11 + 10i$

33. For the following sequence of numbers, $\frac{1}{2}$, $\frac{1}{12}$, $\frac{1}{30}$, ..., the next number will be

(A) $\frac{1}{36}$.

(D) $\frac{1}{56}$.

(B) $\frac{1}{27}$.

(E) $\frac{1}{72}$.

(C) $\frac{1}{48}$.

34. In the right triangle below, determine the measure of $\angle A$ and $\angle B$.

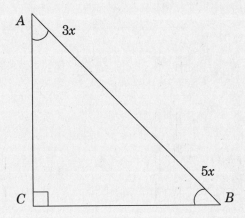

(A) 22.50, 67.50

(D) 11.25, 78.75

(B) 30.00, 60.00

(E) None of the above.

(C) 33.75, 56.25

35. If $m \neq 0$, then $(25)^{3m}(125)^{8m}(5)^m$ can be expressed as

(A) 125^{12m}.

(D) 25^{12m}.

(B) 5^{20m}.

(E) 5^{31m}.

(C) 5^{19m}.

36. If two adjacent corners of a square are at points $P(3, 1)$ and $Q(6, 5)$, how long is its diagonal?

(A) $\dfrac{5}{2}$

(D) 5

(B) $5\sqrt{2}$

(E) $3\sqrt{5}$

(C) 25

37. In the triangle shown below, $\cos\omega$ is equal to

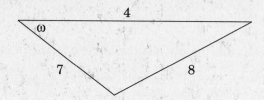

(A) $\dfrac{1}{16}$.

(D) $\dfrac{\sqrt{3}}{3}$.

(B) $\dfrac{\sqrt{2}}{2}$.

(E) $\dfrac{1}{56}$.

(C) $\dfrac{1}{28}$.

For Problems 38 and 39, refer to the following set of numbers.

{9, 21.3, 7.1, 5, 9, 14, 11.2, 17, 12}

38. What is the mean of the set of numbers?

(A) 21.3

(D) 9.0

(B) 105.6

(E) 11.2

(C) 11.7

39. What is the median of the set?

(A) 21.3

(D) 9.0

(B) 105.6

(E) 11.2

(C) 11.7

40. The equation for the set of all points equidistant from the points (2, 6) and (3, 9) is

    (A) $y = 5x - 4$.

    (B) $y = -8x + 4$.

    (C) $y = -3x + 15$.

    (D) $y = -7x + 8$.

    (E) $y = \frac{3}{2}x + 3$.

41. Given the triangle below, what is the value of θ?

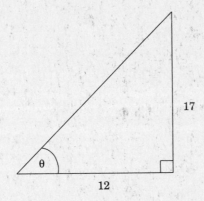

    (A) 54.8°

    (B) 35.2°

    (C) 45.0°

    (D) 42.8°

    (E) 59.2°

42. The roots of $x^2 + 2x + 5 = 0$ are

    (A) 3, 4 .

    (B) $-1 \pm 2i$.

    (C) $3 \pm 4i$.

    (D) 6, 3 .

    (E) $2 \pm 3i$.

43. In the accompanying figure of a circle centered about point O, the measure of arc AB is $\frac{\pi}{5}$ radians. Find $\angle OBA$.

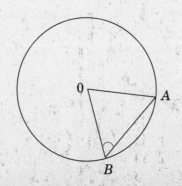

(A) 36°

(D) 72°

(B) 144°

(E) 17°

(C) 90°

44. How many games would it take a baseball coach to try every possible batting order with his nine players?

(A) 9

(D) 362,880

(B) 45

(E) 3.8742×10^8

(C) 81

45. John borrowed $10,000 from his father and insisted on paying it back with 6% simple interest. If he ended up paying $13,000, how long did it take him to pay it off?

(A) 21.667 months

(D) 5 years

(B) 36 months

(E) 6 years

(C) 4 years

46.

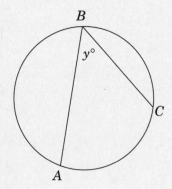

If m $\overset{\frown}{ABC}$ is $\dfrac{3}{2}\pi$ radians, then y is equal to

(A) 90°.

(D) 53°.

(B) 72°.

(E) 45°.

(C) 36°.

47. If $y = 3t + 8$ and $x = 9t$, at what value of x will the graph of this function, in the x-y plane, cross the x-axis?

(A) 20

(D) –24

(B) 16

(E) 48

(C) –8

48. If we double the radius of a sphere, the volume of the sphere is increased by a factor of

(A) 2.

(D) 10.

(B) 6.

(E) 16.

(C) 8.

49. A rectangular piece of metal has an area of 35m^2 and a perimeter of 24m. Which of the following are possible dimensions of the piece?

(A) $\dfrac{35}{2}$ m $\times$ 2m

(D) 6m $\times$ 6m

(B) 5m $\times$ 7m

(E) 8m $\times$ 4m

(C) 35m $\times$ 1m

50. If $f(x) = 2x^2 + 4$ and $g(x) = x - 3$, what number satisfies the expression $f(x) = f(g(x))$?

(A) $\dfrac{3}{2}$

(D) 4

(B) 5

(E) 10

(C) $\dfrac{3}{4}$

TEST 1

ANSWER KEY

1. (C)	14. (A)	27. (C)	40. (C)
2. (B)	15. (A)	28. (D)	41. (A)
3. (D)	16. (B)	29. (D)	42. (B)
4. (B)	17. (D)	30. (A)	43. (D)
5. (B)	18. (C)	31. (A)	44. (D)
6. (A)	19. (C)	32. (B)	45. (D)
7. (D)	20. (D)	33. (D)	46. (E)
8. (E)	21. (E)	34. (C)	47. (D)
9. (C)	22. (E)	35. (E)	48. (C)
10. (D)	23. (C)	36. (B)	49. (B)
11. (B)	24. (C)	37. (E)	50. (A)
12. (E)	25. (A)	38. (C)	
13. (E)	26. (E)	39. (E)	

DETAILED EXPLANATIONS
OF ANSWERS

1. **(C)**

The total John earns is 30 hrs × \$6/hr = \$180. The federal government takes 24%, and the state takes $\frac{1}{4}$ of the 24%, or 6%.

Calculator:

180 $\boxed{-}$ 180 $\boxed{\times}$ .24 $\boxed{-}$ 180 $\boxed{\times}$ .06 $\boxed{=}$ 126

2. **(B)**

$$\frac{7}{3}x = (a^4 + 1)^3$$

Substituting $a = -1$, we obtain

$$\frac{7}{3}x = (1+1)^3 = 8 \ .$$

Multiplying both sides by $\frac{3}{7}$, we solve the equation for x, i.e., $x = \frac{24}{7}$.

3. **(D)**

Three consecutive integers would be x, $x + 1$, and $x + 2$. So

$$x + (x + 1) + (x + 2) = 1,494$$
$$3x + 3 = 1,494$$

Calculator:

1494 $\boxed{-}$ 3 $\boxed{=}$ $\boxed{\div}$ 3 $\boxed{=}$ 497

The smallest integer is 497, followed by $x + 1 = 498$, and $x + 2 = 499$.

4. **(B)**

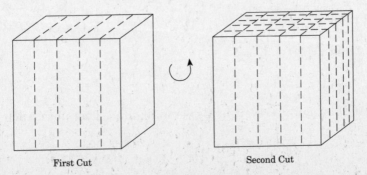

First Cut   Second Cut

Four cuts make five areas done twice.

$5 \times 5 = 25$ rectangular solids with dimensions $5' \times 1' \times 1'$.

5.   **(B)**

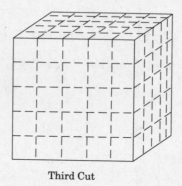

Third Cut

By making the third set of cuts, you end up with 5^3.

Calculator:

5 $\boxed{y^x}$ 3 $\boxed{=}$ 125 congruent cubes.

6.   **(A)**

Using the quadratic formula:

$$x = \frac{7 \pm \sqrt{(7)^2 - 4\,(1)\,(10)}}{2\,(1)}$$

Calculator:

7 $\boxed{x^2}$ $\boxed{-}$ 4 $\boxed{\times}$ 1 $\boxed{\times}$ 10 $\boxed{=}$ $\boxed{\sqrt{}}$ 3

so $x = \dfrac{7 \pm 3}{2}$

$x = 2$ and $x = 5$

By factoring:

$x^2 - 7x + 10 = 0$

$(x - 5)\,(x - 2) = 0$

$x = 5$ and $x = 2$

7.   **(D)**

Since $\triangle ACD$ is equilateral, it is also equiangular. Therefore, each angle is equal to $60°$.

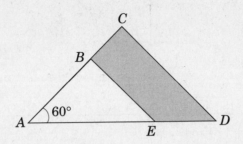

$$\text{Area } \triangle ACD = \quad \left(\overline{AC}\right)^2 \times \sin 60°$$

$$= \frac{1}{2}\,(10)^2 \times \sin 60°$$

$$= \frac{100}{2} \times \frac{\sqrt{3}}{2}$$

$$= 25\sqrt{3}$$

$$\text{Area } \triangle ABE = \frac{1}{2}\left(\overline{AB}\right)^2 \times \sin 60°$$

$$= \frac{1}{2}\,(8)^2 \times \sin 60°$$

$$= \frac{64}{2} \times \frac{\sqrt{3}}{2}$$

$$= 16\sqrt{3}$$

$$\text{Area } BCDE = \text{Area } \triangle ACE - \text{Area } \triangle ABE$$

$$= 25\sqrt{3} - 16\sqrt{3} = 9\sqrt{3}$$

8. **(E)**

$$f(x) = 7x^2 + 3$$

$$g(x) = 2x - 9$$

Substituting 2 into $f(x)$:

$$f(2) = 7(2)^2 + 3 = 31\,.$$

So $g(f(2)) = g(31)$.

Substituting and solving:

$$g(31) = 2(31) - 9 = 53\,.$$

9. **(C)**

Slope $= \dfrac{y_2 - y_1}{x_2 - x_1}$ $\quad A\,(-5,\,3) \quad C\,(1,\,-3)$

Calculator:

3 $\boxed{+/-}$ $\boxed{-}$ 3 $\boxed{=}$ $\boxed{\div}$ $\boxed{(\,)}$ 1 $\boxed{-}$ 5 $\boxed{+/-}$ $\boxed{(\,)}$ $\boxed{=}$ -1

10. **(D)**

Slope $= \dfrac{y_2 - y_1}{x_2 - x_1}$ $\quad B\,(4,\,5) \quad C\,(1,\,-3)$

Calculator:

3 $\boxed{+/-}$ $\boxed{-}$ 5 $\boxed{=}$ $\boxed{\div}$ $\boxed{(\,)}$ 1 $\boxed{-}$ 4 $\boxed{(\,)}$ $\boxed{=}$ 2.667

11. **(B)**

Distance formula, $d = \sqrt{(x_1 - x_2)^2 + (y_1 - y_2)^2}$ $\quad A\,(-5,\,3) \quad D\,(-4,\,-3)$

Calculator:

5 $\boxed{+/-}$ $\boxed{-}$ 4 $\boxed{+/-}$ $\boxed{=}$ $\boxed{x^2}$ $\boxed{+}$ $\boxed{(\,)}$ 3 $\boxed{-}$ 3 $\boxed{+/-}$ $\boxed{(\,)}$ $\boxed{x^2}$ $\boxed{=}$ $\boxed{\sqrt{}}$ 6.083

12. **(E)**

$2x + 3y = 6$

$y - 2 = \dfrac{-2x}{3}$

Multiplying the second equation by 3, we obtain

$$3y - 6 = -2x\,.$$

Transposing, we obtain

$$2x + 3y = 6\,.$$

Thus, both equations are equivalent and define one straight line. Since they intersect at every point, there are an infinite number of solutions.

13. **(E)**

Using the quadratic formula, $x = \dfrac{-4 \pm \sqrt{(4)^2 - 4\,(1)\,(6)}}{2\,(1)}$. Simplifying the term under the radical

Calculator:

$4 \boxed{x^2} \boxed{-} 4 \boxed{\times} 1 \boxed{\times} 6 \boxed{=} -8 \boxed{\sqrt{\ }}$ which gives you an error because a negative number is under the radical. Therefore, the answer is **(E)**, no real roots.

14. **(A)**

$y < -x + 3$

$y < x - 3$

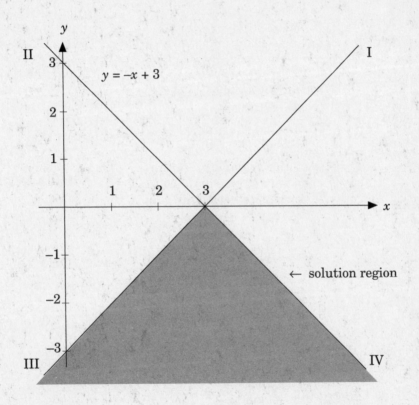

Note that the solution to the system of inequalities lies in quadrants III and IV.

15. **(A)**

Ratio: $\dfrac{25}{16} = \dfrac{\pi r_1^2}{\pi r_2^2}$; $\dfrac{25}{16} = \dfrac{r_1^2}{r_2^2}$

Taking the square root: $\dfrac{5}{4} = \dfrac{r_1}{r_2}$

Multiply both sides by r_2: $r_1 = \dfrac{5}{4}(r_2)$

Double both sides: $2r_1 = \dfrac{5}{4}(2r_2)$

$$d_1 = \dfrac{5}{4}d_2 \Rightarrow d_1 \text{ is } \dfrac{5}{4} \text{ as large as } d_2.$$

16.   **(B)**

In order for a rectangle to encompass the greatest area, all of its sides must be equal. If this is the case, its perimeter $p = 4S$ and its area $A = S^2$. We were given that its perimeter $p = 52$m. Substituting, we get $4S = 52$m or $S = 13$m. Substituting into the area formula, we get $A = (13\text{m})^2 = 169\text{m}^2$.

17.   **(D)**

When two parallel line segments are cut by another segment, their alternate interior angles must be equal. These angles are listed in Statement II. The other criteria given are irrelevant to the problem.

18.   **(C)**

The surface area of a sphere is $4\pi r^2$. Solving for the radius, we obtain

$$r = \sqrt{\dfrac{64\pi\text{m}^2}{4\pi}} = 4\text{m} .$$

The volume of a sphere is $\dfrac{4}{3}\pi r^3$.

Thus, $V = \left(\dfrac{4}{3}\right)\pi(4\text{m})^3 = \dfrac{256}{3}\pi\text{m}^3 .$

Half of this volume is $\dfrac{128}{3}\pi\text{m}^3 .$

19.   **(C)**

The equation for the interior angles of an n-sided regular polygon is $180\,(n-2)$, where n is the number of sides.

Calculator:

$180 \boxed{\times} \boxed{(} 9 \boxed{-} 2 \boxed{)} \boxed{=} 1260$

If you do not know the formula, you can break down the figure into seven triangles (which is $n - 2$) and multiply by 180° (the number of degrees in the sum of angles of a triangle).

20. **(D)**

$C_1 = 2\pi(r)$

Calculator:

$2 \boxed{\times} \boxed{\pi} \boxed{\times} 5 \boxed{=} 31.415927$

$C_2 = 2C_1 = 2\pi(r_2)$

Calculator:

$2 \boxed{\times} 31.415927 \boxed{=} 62.831853$

$r_2 = \dfrac{C_2}{2\pi}$

Calculator:

$62.831853 \boxed{\div} \boxed{(\,)} 2 \boxed{\times} \boxed{\pi} \boxed{(\,)} \boxed{=} 10$

21. **(E)**

A function is defined as having a unique y value for every x value. Statements II and III satisfy this criterion.

Statement I is a hyperbola, which may have two range values for each value in the domain.

22. **(E)**

$3x - 18 = 2x + 5$ since vertical angles are equal. Simplifying, $x = 23$. Then substitute that into $3x - 18$.

Calculator:

$3 \boxed{\times} 23 \boxed{-} 18 \boxed{=} 51$

23. **(C)**

$f(-20) = -1$

Substituting: $g(f(-20)) = g(-1) = -2$

Squaring: $[g(-1)]^2 = 4$

$g(1) = 4$

Subtracting: $[g(f(-20))]^2 - g(1) = 4 - 4 = 0$

24.   **(C)**

$A_1 = \pi r_1^2$

Calculator:

$\boxed{\pi}$ $\boxed{\times}$ 5 $\boxed{x^2}$ $\boxed{=}$ 78.539816

$A_2 = 2A_1 = \pi r_2^2$

Calculator:

2 $\boxed{\times}$ 78.539816 $\boxed{=}$ 157.07963

$r_2 = \sqrt{\dfrac{A_2}{\pi}}$

Calculator:

157.07963 $\boxed{\div}$ $\boxed{\pi}$ $\boxed{=}$ $\boxed{\sqrt{}}$ 7.0710678

25.   **(A)**

Let x = the speed of the wind.

$300 - x$ = the speed of the plane relative to the ground.

Since speed × time = distance, solve for x.

$$(300 - x)(2) = 200$$
$$600 - 2x = 200$$
$$2x = 400$$
$$x = 200 \text{ mph}$$

26.   **(E)**

The sine of angle C is $\dfrac{1}{2}$. The altitude $\overline{BD}$ is thus

$$\overline{BD} = \overline{BC} \, \sin C = 8\left(\frac{1}{2}\right) = 4.$$

Length $\overline{DC}$ is found from the Pythagorean theorem: $a^2 + b^2 = c^2$:

$$(\overline{DC})^2 = (\overline{BC})^2 - (\overline{BD})^2$$
$$(\overline{DC})^2 = (8)^2 - (4)^2 = 48$$
$$\overline{DC} = 4\sqrt{3}$$

Area of $\triangle DBC = \dfrac{1}{2}(\overline{DC})(\overline{BD}) = \dfrac{1}{2}(4\sqrt{3})(4) = 8\sqrt{3}$. Angle C must be $30°$,

since its sine is $\dfrac{1}{2}$. Therefore, angle A is $60°$. We must first find side AB:

$$\sin 60° = \dfrac{4}{AB}; \quad AB = \dfrac{4\,(2)}{\sqrt{3}} = \dfrac{8\sqrt{3}}{3}$$

Length $AD = (AB)(\cos 60°) = \left(\dfrac{8\sqrt{3}}{3}\right)\left(\dfrac{1}{2}\right) = \dfrac{4\sqrt{3}}{3}$

Area $\triangle ABD = \dfrac{1}{2}(\text{base})(\text{altitude}) = \dfrac{1}{2}(AD)(BD)$

$$= \left(\dfrac{1}{2}\right)\left(\dfrac{4\sqrt{3}}{3}\right)(4) = \dfrac{8\sqrt{3}}{3}$$

The ratio of the two areas is

$$\dfrac{\text{Area } \triangle ABD}{\text{Area } \triangle DBC} = \dfrac{\dfrac{8\sqrt{3}}{3}}{8\sqrt{3}} = \dfrac{1}{3}.$$

27.　　**(C)**

The total number of possible combinations on a pair of dice is $(6)^2 = 36$ combinations.

We are looking for combinations where the number showing on the red die exceeds the number on the green die by 2. This occurs only for the following combinations.

Red	Green
3	1
4	2
5	3
6	4

Thus, there are four combinations that satisfy the constraints, out of 36 possible combinations.

The probability is equal to $\dfrac{4}{36} = \dfrac{1}{9}$.

28.   **(D)**

The given equation is $x^2 + y^2 - 6x + 8y = 0$. In order to find the center, we must complete the square:

$$(x^2 - 6x + a_1) + (y^2 + 8y + a_2) = 0 + a_1 + a_2$$

To complete the square of a term defined by $x^2 + ax$, we add $\left(\dfrac{a}{2}\right)^2$ to both sides.

For the first term, we add 9 to both sides. For the second term, we add 16 to both sides. The resulting equation is

$$(x^2 - 6x + 9) + (y^2 + 8y + 16) = 25 .$$

This is equivalent to

$$(x - 3)^2 + (y + 4)^2 = 25 .$$

This is the equation of a circle with center $(3, -4)$.

29.   **(D)**

The inequality $|\, 2 - 5x\, | < 3$ may be rewritten as

$$-3 < 2 - 5x < 3 .$$

Subtracting 2 from each side, we obtain

$$-5 < -5x < 1 .$$

Dividing by -5 gives

$$-\frac{1}{5} < x < 1 .$$

This is the interval over which all solutions lie. We are looking for an interval that does not contain any solutions to the inequality. The only interval given in the choices that satisfies this criterion is

$$-\frac{3}{5} < x < -\frac{1}{2} .$$

30.   **(A)**

Being that $\sec\alpha$ is $\dfrac{17}{15}$, we recognize α as an angle within an 8-15-17 right triangle:

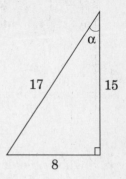

$$\sec\alpha = \frac{\text{hyp}}{\text{adj}}$$

Figure 1

We note, for the same reason, that β is an angle within a 6-8-10 right triangle:

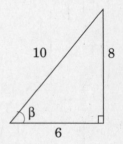

$$\cos\beta = \frac{\text{adj}}{\text{hyp}}$$

Figure 2

In order to find sin (α + β), we use the identity

$$\sin(\alpha + \beta) = \sin\alpha\cos\beta + \cos\alpha\,\sin\beta.$$

From Figure 1, we see that $\sin\alpha = \dfrac{8}{17}$ and $\cos\alpha = \dfrac{15}{17}$. From Figure 2, we see that $\sin\beta = \dfrac{8}{10}$ and $\cos\beta = \dfrac{6}{10}$. Next we substitute into the formula:

$$\sin(\alpha + \beta) = \sin\alpha\cos\beta + \cos\alpha\,\sin\beta$$

$$= \left(\frac{8}{17}\right)\left(\frac{6}{10}\right) + \left(\frac{15}{17}\right)\left(\frac{8}{10}\right)$$

$$= \frac{168}{170} = \frac{84}{85}$$

31.   **(A)**

The relation for the volume of a hollow cone is

$$V = \frac{1}{3}\pi r^2 h.$$

Substituting the values given for V and h, we obtain

$$81\pi m^3 = \frac{1}{3}\pi r^2 3m, \text{ or } 81m^2 = r^2.$$

Solving for r yields $r = 9m$.

$$\text{Total mass} = \text{weight} \times \text{surface area}$$
$$\text{Weight} = 2 \text{ kg/m}^2$$

$$\text{Surface area} = \pi r \sqrt{r^2 + h^2}$$

$$= \pi \,(9m) \,\sqrt{(9m)^2 + (3m)^2}$$

$$= \pi \,(9m) \,\sqrt{81m^2 + 9m^2}$$

$$= \pi \,(9m) \,\sqrt{90m^2}$$

$$= \pi \,(9m) \,(3m) \,\sqrt{10}$$

$$= 27m^2\pi \,\sqrt{10}$$

$$\text{Total mass} = (2 \text{ kg/m}^2) \,(27m^2\pi \,\sqrt{10})$$

$$= 54\pi \,\sqrt{10} \text{ kg}$$

32.   **(B)**

$$f(z) = z^2 + 3z + 5$$

$f(2 + i)$ is obtained by substituting $(2 + i)$ for z:

$$f(2 + i) = (2 + i)^2 + 3(2 + i) + 5$$

Multiplying out:

$$f(2 + i) = 4 + 4i - 1 + 6 + 3i + 5$$
$$f(2 + i) = 14 + 7i$$

33.   **(D)**

To determine the next number, we look for a pattern among the previous terms. Only the denominators differ. We note by inspection that each denominator is equal to the product of two successive integers. For example, the first term: $\dfrac{1}{2} = \dfrac{1}{1 \times 2}$

the second term: $\dfrac{1}{12} = \dfrac{1}{3 \times 4}$

the third term: $\dfrac{1}{30} = \dfrac{1}{5 \times 6}$

Thus, the next term in the sequence can be expected to be

$$\dfrac{1}{7 \times 8} \text{ or } \dfrac{1}{56}.$$

34.   **(C)**

Since $\angle A + \angle B = 90°$, then $3x + 5x = 90$ or $8x = 90$,

Calculator:

$90 \boxed{\div} 8 \boxed{=} 11.25$

$\angle A = 3 \boxed{\times} 11.25 \boxed{=} 33.75$

$\angle B = 5 \boxed{\times} 11.25 \boxed{=} 56.25$

35.   **(E)**

We use the laws of exponents to solve this problem. $(25)^{3m}$ can be expressed as $(5^2)^{3m}$, which can also be written as 5^{6m}.

$(125)^{8m}$ can, by similar argument, be expressed as 5^{24m}.

When we multiply a number of the same base raised to different powers, we simply keep the same base and add the exponents. Thus:

$$(25)^{3m} (125)^{8m} (5)^m = 5^{6m} 5^{24m} (5)^m = 5^{31m}$$

36.   **(B)**

From the two points given, the fact that they are adjacent corners of a square allows us to find the side of the square. Using the distance formula,

$$d = \sqrt{(x_2 - x_1)^2 + (y_2 - y_1)^2} \,,$$

and substituting points P and Q, we obtain

$$d = \sqrt{(6-3)^2 + (5-1)^2} \,,$$

or $\qquad d = \sqrt{25} = 5$.

Thus, the side is 5.

We may find the diagonal by using the Pythagorean theorem: $a^2 + b^2 = c^2$.

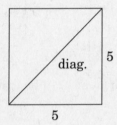

We apply it to the triangle formed by the diagonal.

$$\text{diagonal}^2 = 5^2 + 5^2$$

$$\text{diagonal}^2 = 50$$

$$\text{diagonal} = \sqrt{50} = 5\sqrt{2}$$

37.   **(E)**

To solve, we use the law of cosines:

$$c^2 = a^2 + b^2 - 2ab\cos(\text{included angle}).$$

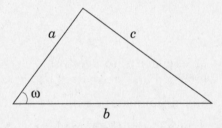

In the figure given, $a = 4$, $b = 7$, $c = 8$, and ω is the included angle.

We solve the law of cosine relation for $\cos\omega$:

$$c^2 = a^2 + b^2 - 2ab\cos\omega.$$

Transposing a^2 and b^2 and dividing through by $-2ab$, we obtain:

$$\frac{c^2 - a^2 - b^2}{-2ab} = \cos\omega.$$

Substituting for a, b, and c we obtain

$$\cos\omega = \frac{8^2 - 4^2 - 7^2}{-2\,(4)\,(7)} = \frac{64 - 16 - 49}{-56} = \frac{-1}{-56} = \frac{1}{56}.$$

38.   **(C)**

Mean is the average $\dfrac{\Sigma n}{\#}$.

Calculator:

$$9 \boxed{+} 21.3 \boxed{+} 7.1 \boxed{+} 5 \boxed{+} 9 \boxed{+} 14 \boxed{+} 11.2 \boxed{+} 17 \boxed{+} 12 \boxed{=} \boxed{\div} 9 \boxed{=}$$

$$11.733 \approx 11.7$$

39.   **(E)**

Median is the middle number when the set of numbers is arranged in ascending order which would be 11.2.

40.   **(C)**

The two given points P (2, 6) and Q (3, 9) determine a line segment. The set of all points which are equidistant from these points is known as the locus and is equivalent to the perpendicular bisector of $\overline{PQ}$. This perpendicular bisector is a line, name it L, and can therefore be fully described by an equation. A convenient way to obtain this equation is by employing the point-slope form of an equation.

We can find a point on L simply by finding the midpoint of $\overline{PQ}$, because this point is equidistant from both P and Q by definition. Substituting points P and Q in the midpoint formula,

$$x_m = \frac{x_2 + x_1}{2}, \qquad y_m = \frac{y_2 + y_1}{2},$$

we obtain

$$x_m = \frac{3 + 2}{2}, \qquad y_m = \frac{9 + 6}{2}$$

$$(x_m, y_m) = \left(\frac{5}{2}, \frac{15}{2}\right).$$

Since L must be perpendicular to $\overline{PQ}$, the slope m_1 of L and the slope m_2 of $\overline{PQ}$ must satisfy the relation

$$m_1 m_2 = -1.$$

Recall that the slope m of a line with points (x_1, y_1) and (x_2, y_2) is given by

$$\frac{y_2 - y_1}{x_2 - x_1}.$$

So the slope of $\overline{PQ}$, m_2, is given by

$$m_2 = \frac{9-6}{3-2} = \frac{3}{1} = 3.$$

Since $3\left(-\frac{1}{3}\right) = -1$, the slope of L is $-\frac{1}{3}$.

Notice that we have now obtained not only the slope of line L but also a point on L, so we may use the point-slope form of an equation to obtain an equation for L. This form is given by

$$y - y_1 = m(x - x_1) \,.$$

Substituting, we obtain

$$y - \frac{15}{2} = -\frac{1}{3}\left(x - \frac{5}{2}\right) \quad \text{or} \quad y = -\frac{1}{3}x + \frac{25}{3}.$$

41.   **(A)**

$$\tan\theta = \frac{\text{opp}}{\text{adj}}, \text{ so } \theta = \tan^{-1}\left(\frac{\text{opp}}{\text{adj}}\right) \Rightarrow$$

Calculator:

17 ÷ 12 = inv tan 54.80

42.   **(B)**

The polynomial is not factorable, so we must use the quadratic formula:

$$x = \frac{-b \pm \sqrt{b^2 - 4ac}}{2a}$$

In the polynomial $a = 1$, $b = 2$, $c = 5$. Substituting, we get

$$x = \frac{-2 \pm \sqrt{2^2 - 4\,(1)\,(5)}}{2\,(1)}.$$

Simplifying:

$$x = \frac{-2 \pm \sqrt{-16}}{2} = \frac{-2 \pm 4\sqrt{-1}}{2} = -1 \pm 2\sqrt{-1}\,.$$

We know $\sqrt{-1} = i$, so

$$x = -1 \pm 2i\,.$$

43.   **(D)**

From a theorem, we know that a central angle is equal in measurement to the arc it intercepts. The arc measurement is given as

$$m \stackrel{\frown}{AB} = \frac{1}{5} \pi \text{ radians.}$$

Converting this to degrees, we obtain

$$\left(\frac{1}{5}\pi\right)\left(\frac{180}{\pi}\right) = 36° .$$

Note that points *A*, *O*, and *B* form a triangle. Two sides of this triangle are equal to the radius of the circle. Thus, they are equal sides, and Δ*AOB* is isosceles (we know that the base angles of an isosceles triangle are equal). The vertex angle is 36°, and there are 180° in a triangle. The relation that is set up is

$$36° + 2 \text{ (base angle)} = 180° .$$

Solving for the base angle:

$$\text{base angle} = \frac{180° - 36°}{2} = 72° .$$

Thus, ∠*OBA* = 72°.

44.   **(D)**

This is the possible combinations of nine items which is *n*! (*n*-factorial). Most scientific calculators have a $\boxed{x!}$ button. Otherwise, the factorial formula is $9 \times 8 \times 7 \times 6 \times 5 \times 4 \times 3 \times 2 \times 1 = 362{,}880$.

45.   **(D)**

Since *I* = *PRT* and the interest is 13,000 – 10,000 or 3,000, then $T = \dfrac{I}{PR}$.

Calculator:

3000 $\boxed{\div}$ $\boxed{(}$ 10000 $\boxed{\times}$ .06 $\boxed{)}$ $\boxed{=}$ 5 years

46.   **(E)**

From a theorem we know that the measure of an inscribed angle is equal to $\dfrac{1}{2}$ the intercepted arc.

We are told that $m \stackrel{\frown}{ABC}$ is $\dfrac{3}{2}\pi$ radians. There are 2π radians in a circle. Therefore, the intercepted arc is the remaining $\dfrac{\pi}{2}$ radians.

Converting to degrees:

$$\left(\frac{\pi}{2}\right)\left(\frac{180}{\pi}\right) = 90° \ .$$

The angle y is half of this:

$$y = \frac{90°}{2} = 45° \ .$$

47. **(D)**

We first have to obtain y as a function of x. We note by inspection that y is equivalent to one-third of x increased by 8:

$$y = 3t + 8 = \left(\frac{1}{3}\right)9t + 8 = \frac{1}{3}x + 8 \ .$$

This is the equation we need to obtain the x-intercept. Setting y to 0 and solving for x'

$$0 = \frac{1}{3}x + 8$$

$$-8 = \frac{1}{3}x$$

$$-24 = x$$

48. **(C)**

The volume of a sphere is a function of its radius

$$V = \frac{4}{3}\pi r^3 \ .$$

Let the radius $= r_1$.

Doubling this, we get: $r_2 = 2r_1$.

The initial volume is $V_1 = \frac{4}{3}\pi r_1^3$.

The volume after doubling the radius is $V_2 = \frac{4}{3}\pi r_2^3$.

Substituting $2r_1$ for r_2, we have:

$$V_2 = \frac{4}{3}\pi(2r_1)^3$$

$$= \frac{4}{3}\pi(2)^3 r_1^3 \qquad \text{(from the laws of exponents)}$$

$$= \frac{4}{3}\pi 8 r_1^3$$

$$= 8\left(\frac{4}{3}\pi r_1^3\right)$$

$$= 8V_1$$

Thus, the volume is increased by a factor of 8.

49.　　**(B)**

The shape given is a rectangle. Its area is equal to the length multiplied by the width.

The perimeter is twice the length plus twice the width.

Let x = length, y = width. The relevant equations are

$$xy = 35\text{m}^2 \tag{1}$$

$$2x + 2y = 24\text{m} \tag{2}$$

Rewriting equation (1): $y = \dfrac{35\text{m}^2}{x}$.

Substituting for y in equation (2):

$$2x + 2\left(\frac{35\text{m}^2}{x}\right) = 24\text{m} \ .$$

Multiplying by x:

$$2x^2 + 70\text{m}^2 = 24x\text{m} \ .$$

Subtracting $24x$m from both sides:

$$2x^2 - 24x\text{m} + 70\text{m}^2 = 0 \ .$$

Dividing all terms by 2:

$$x^2 - 12x\text{m} + 35\text{m}^2 = 0.$$

This can be factored into:

$$(x - 7\text{m})(x - 5\text{m}) = 0 \ .$$

From this we get

$$x - 5\text{m} = 0 \ \text{ or } \ x - 7\text{m} = 0 \ .$$

Two possible lengths are

$$x = 5\text{m}, \ x = 7\text{m}.$$

Substituting back into equation (1):

$$(5\text{m})y = 35\text{m}^2 \Rightarrow y = 7\text{m}$$

$$(7\text{m})y = 35\text{m}^2 \Rightarrow y = 5\text{m}$$

Thus, the possible dimensions are are

$$5\text{m} \times 7\text{m} \ \text{ and } \ 7\text{m} \times 5\text{m}.$$

$5\text{m} \times 7\text{m}$ are the only dimensions that correspond to the choices.

50. **(A)**

To solve, we equate the expressions for $f(x)$ and $f(g(x))$.

$$f(x) = 2x^2 + 4 \quad \text{(Given):}$$

$$f(g(x)) = 2(x-3)^2 + 4$$

$$= 2(x^2 - 6x + 9) + 4$$

$$= 2x^2 - 12x + 22$$

The necessary equation is

$$2x^2 + 4 = 2x^2 - 12x + 22 \ .$$

Subtracting $2x^2$ from both sides

$$4 = -12x + 22 \ .$$

Transposing $-12x$ and 4 to opposite sides:

$$12x = 18 \ .$$

Solving for x:

$$x = \frac{18}{12} = \frac{3}{2} \ .$$

THE SAT SUBJECT TEST IN

Math
Level 1

PRACTICE TEST 2

SAT Mathematics Level 1

Practice Test 2

Time: 1 Hour
50 Questions

DIRECTIONS: Choose the best answer for each question and mark the letter of your selection on the corresponding answer sheet.

NOTES:

(1) Some questions require the use of a calculator. You must decide when the use of your calculator will be helpful.

(2) Make sure your calculator is in degree mode.

(3) All figures are drawn to scale and lie in a plane unless otherwise stated.

(4) The domain of any function f is the set of all real numbers x for which $f(x)$ is a real number, unless other information is provided.

REFERENCE INFORMATION: The following information may be helpful in answering some of the questions.

Volume of a right circular cone with radius r and height h
$$V = \frac{1}{3}\pi r^2 h$$

Lateral area of a right circular cone with circumference c and slant height l
$$S = \frac{1}{2}cl$$

Volume of a sphere with radius r
$$V = \frac{4}{3}\pi r^3$$

Surface area of a sphere with radius r
$$S = 4\pi r^2$$

Volume of a pyramid with base area B and height h
$$V = \frac{1}{3}Bh$$

1. What is the probability of drawing an ace from a well-shuffled deck of 52 cards?

    (A) 0.0769

    (B) 0.0192

    (C) 0.0196

    (D) 0.0385

    (E) 0.5000

2. The simplest expression for $\dfrac{a^2 - 3ab + 2b^2}{2b^2 + ab - a^2}$ is

    (A) 1.

    (B) $a + b$.

    (C) $\dfrac{2a+b}{b-a}$.

    (D) $a - b$.

    (E) $\dfrac{b-a}{b+a}$.

3. What is the range of values for which $|\,6x - 5\,| \le 8$ is satisfied?

    (A) $-\dfrac{1}{2} \le x \le \dfrac{1}{2}$

    (B) $0 \le x \le \dfrac{5}{6}$

    (C) $-1 \le x \le \dfrac{1}{2}$

    (D) $-\dfrac{1}{2} \le x \le \dfrac{13}{6}$

    (E) $-\dfrac{1}{2} \le x \le \dfrac{1}{3}$

4. The diagonals of a rhombus are 12 and 18, what is the area of the rhombus?

    (A) 54 square units

    (B) 78 square units

    (C) 156 square units

    (D) 216 square units

    (E) 108 square units

5. Two circles with radii of 5 and centers X and Y, respectively, are both tangent to $\overleftrightarrow{RS}$ as shown at R and S. If $\overline{RS}$ is 24 and Z is the midpoint, what is the length of $\overline{XY}$?

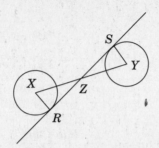

(A) 21.82

(D) 26

(B) 24.515

(E) 10.909

(C) 13

6. The coordinates of the vertices of a right triangle are (1, 3), (5, 3), and (1, 6). Find the slope of its hypotenuse.

(A) $-\dfrac{3}{4}$

(D) $-\dfrac{1}{4}$

(B) $-\dfrac{5}{3}$

(E) −2

(C) $\dfrac{4}{3}$

7. An airplane at an altitude of 3,000 feet is descending at an angle of 25°. How far will the plane travel before it lands?

(A) 2,719.0 feet

(D) 7,098.6 feet

(B) 1,268.0 feet

(E) 3,310.1 feet

(C) 6,433.5 feet

8. The force of attraction of two bodies is given by the equation $F = \dfrac{Gm_1m_2}{r^2}$; where $G = 6.6726 \times 10^{-11}$ m³/kgs² and r is the distance between them. What is the force of attraction between Earth (mass $m_1 = 5.98 \times 10^{24}$ kg) and the moon ($m_2 = 7.36 \times 10^{22}$ kg) if they are separated by 3.84×10^8 meters?

(A) 1.99×10^{20}

(D) 1.99×10^{42}

(B) 7.65×10^{28}

(E) 5.2×10^{11}

(C) 5.02×10^{71}

9. In how many different ways can the letters *a*, *b*, *c*, *d* be arranged if they are selected three at a time?

    (A) 8   (D) 4

    (B) 12   (E) 48

    (C) 24

10. Solve the logarithmic equation $\dfrac{\log\,[(25)\,(15)]^2}{\log\,(25)+\log\,(15)}$.

    (A) 2.574   (D) 14.955

    (B) 2.000   (E) Not solvable

    (C) 9.375

11. A man buys a book for $20 and wishes to sell it. What price should he mark on it if he wishes a 40% discount while making a 50% profit on the cost price?

    (A) $25   (D) $50

    (B) $30   (E) $55

    (C) $40

12. If $i = \sqrt{-1}$, then $(a+bi)^2 - (a-bi)^2$ is equivalent to

    (A) $4abi$.   (D) $2bi$.

    (B) -1.   (E) $-2b^2$.

    (C) $a^2 - b^2$.

13. An isosceles triangle has sides 17, 17, 16. What is the tangent of one of its base angles?

    (A) $\dfrac{1}{2}$ (D) $\dfrac{15}{8}$

    (B) $\dfrac{16}{17}$ (E) 1

    (C) $\dfrac{8}{17}$

14. If you took a 10" × 16" piece of plywood and cut out 15 circles with a 3" diameter, approximately how much scrap wood would be left, not taking into account thickness?

(A) 106 sq. in.

(D) 160 sq. in.

(B) 44 sq. in.

(E) 141.4 sq. in.

(C) 54 sq. in.

15. The diagonal of a square has endpoints (3, 8) and (−1, 2). What is its area?

(A) 10

(D) 32

(B) 13

(E) 40

(C) 26

16. If $A * B$ is defined as $(A - B)(A + B)$, what is the value of $6 * (5 * 4)$?

(A) 105

(D) −45

(B) −1,645

(E) 77

(C) −5

17. How many integers are in the solution set of $|3x - 2| > -1$?

(A) None

(D) Three

(B) One

(E) Infinitely many

(C) Two

18. If the polynomial $x^3 + 4x^2 - 3x + 8$ is divided by $x - 5$, the remainder is

(A) 140.

(D) 218.

(B) 175.

(E) 300.

(C) 200.

19. The fraction $\dfrac{\dfrac{2}{b^2 a^2}}{\dfrac{1}{b^2 - 2b}}$ may be expressed more compactly as

(A) $\dfrac{2a}{b}$

(B) $\dfrac{b-4}{b}$

(C) $\dfrac{ab}{b^2 - a}$ (D) $\dfrac{b-a}{a}$

(E) $\dfrac{2b-4}{a^2 b}$

20. If one root of $x^2 - ax + 12 = 0$ is 6, then the other root is

(A) 2.   (D) 8.

(B) −4.   (E) 12.

(C) −6.

21. If the measure of an angle exceeds its complement by 40°, then its measure is

(A) 65°.   (D) 40°.

(B) 50°.   (E) 30°.

(C) 45°.

22. A triangle has angles measuring x, y, and $x + y$. The triangle must be

(A) isosceles.   (D) equilateral.

(B) scalene.   (E) obtuse.

(C) right.

23. In the figure, the line AG is the intersection of plane DAF with

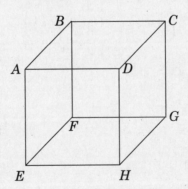

(A) EHC.   (D) EFC.

(B) ABG.   (E) FED.

(C) GFA.

24. A circle is centered at point (3, 4). The endpoints of its diameter are *A* and *B*. The coordinates of point *A* are (−2, 1). What are the coordinates of point *B*?

(A) (6, 3).

(D) (9, 3).

(B) (8, 7).

(E) (5, 8).

(C) (4, 5).

25. What is the solution set of the equation $\cos 2x + 3\sin^2 x - 6\sin x + 4 = 0$?

(A) $\{2n\pi + \dfrac{\pi}{2}\}$ $n = 0, 1, 2, 3, \ldots$

(D) $\{\quad\}$

(B) $\{2n\pi\}$ $n = 0, 1, 2, 3, \ldots$

(E) $\{2n\pi - \dfrac{\pi}{2}\}$ $n = 0, 1, 2, 3, \ldots$

(C) $\{2(n-1)\pi\}$ $n = 0, 1, 2, 3, \ldots$

26. The figure is a sketch of $y = f(x)$. What is $f(f(6))$?

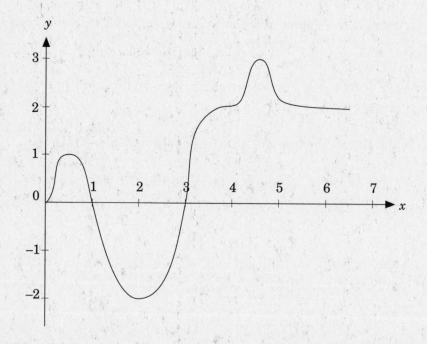

(A) −2

(D) 3

(B) 1

(E) 0

(C) 2

27. If Fahrenheit temperature and Celsius temperature are related through the equation $F = 32 + \dfrac{9}{5}C$; what would 165°F be in Celsius?

    (A) 329°

    (B) 32.011°

    (C) 109.4°

    (D) 133°

    (E) 73.9°

28. A man encloses a rectangular area of 30,000 square feet with 800 feet of fencing. What is the maximum rectangular area he can enclose?

    (A) 60,000

    (B) 55,000

    (C) 50,000

    (D) 40,000

    (E) 72,000

29. If $\log_8 N = \dfrac{2}{3}$, what is the value of N?

    (A) 2

    (B) 4

    (C) 8

    (D) 10

    (E) 12

30. One solution of the equation $27^{x^2+1} = 243$ is

    (A) $\sqrt{5}$.

    (B) $\dfrac{3}{2}$.

    (C) $-\sqrt{\dfrac{2}{3}}$.

    (D) $\dfrac{-5}{2}$.

    (E) 5.

31. In the system $\begin{pmatrix} ax + by = 20 \\ bx + ay = 16 \end{pmatrix}$ the solution is $x = 2$ and $y = 1$. What are the coefficients a and b?

    (A) $a = 2$, $b = 1$

    (B) $a = 8$, $b = 7$

    (C) $a = 8$, $b = 4$

    (D) $a = 7$, $b = 14$

    (E) $a = 9$, $b = 4$

32. If a figure has exterior angles that all measure 72°, then the figure is a

    (A) triangle.   (D) hexagon.

    (B) square.   (E) octagon.

    (C) pentagon.

33. A rhombus has consecutive sides of measure $3x + 10$ and $2x + 15$ with included angle $12x$. What is the length of its shorter diagonal?

    (A) $\dfrac{25}{2}$ (D) 18

    (B) 5   (E) 25

    (C) 10

34. Find the area under the graph below.

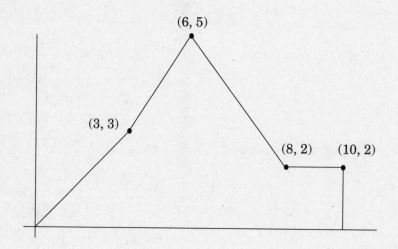

(6, 5)

(3, 3)

(8, 2)   (10, 2)

    (A) 24.5   (D) 21.5

    (B) 27.5   (E) 26.0

    (C) 23.0

35. The function $f(x) = -\mid \sin x \mid$ lies in the quadrant(s)

    (A) I and II.   (D) IV only.

    (B) I and III.   (E) III and IV.

    (C) II and III.

36. A deposit bottle of soda costs 50¢, if the soda costs 30¢ more than the bottle, how much money should you receive by returning the bottle?

    (A) 20¢

    (B) 30¢

    (C) 15¢

    (D) 10¢

    (E) 5¢

37. If $7x = \dfrac{3}{5}x$, then $7 + 2x$ must equal

    (A) $\dfrac{35}{3}$.

    (B) -3.

    (C) 9.

    (D) 7.

    (E) $\dfrac{-32}{5}$.

38. The equation $x^2 + 2x + 7 = 0$ has

    (A) two complex conjugate roots.

    (B) two real rational roots.

    (C) two real equal roots.

    (D) two rational equal roots.

    (E) two real irrational roots.

39. The sum of a two-digit number is 9. The number is equal to 9 times the units digit. Find the number.

    (A) 36

    (B) 45

    (C) 63

    (D) 54

    (E) 72

40. A square of side length 2 units shares a corner with a triangle and its vertices bisect the triangle's sides. What kind of triangle is it and what is the total area?

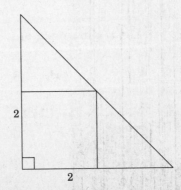

(A) Equilateral; 4   (D) Isosceles; 8

(B) Equilateral; 8   (E) Cannot be determined.

(C) Isosceles; 4

41. In the figure below of a regular hexagon inscribed within a circle with center O and line segment $\overline{AB} = 7$, what is the area of the circle?

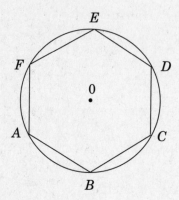

(A) $\left(\dfrac{7}{6}\right)^2 \pi$ (D) 21π

(B) 7π (E) 49π

(C) $\left(\dfrac{7}{2}\right)^2 \pi$

42. At 4:00 in the afternoon a 40 foot flagpole casts a 60 foot shadow. What is the angle of inclination from the end of the shadow to the top of the pole?

(A) 41.8°   (D) 56.3°

(B) 33.7°   (E) 66.3°

(C) 48.2°

43. The equation $x = 3y + 8$ has a y-intercept of

(A) $\dfrac{1}{2}$ (D) -8

(B) 8   (E) 16

(C) $-\dfrac{8}{3}$

44. In the figure, side y is 10 less than x. What is the length of x?

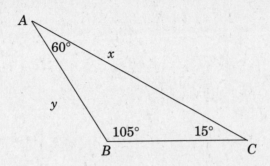

(A) $5 + 5\sqrt{3}$

(D) 25

(B) $\dfrac{\sqrt{3}}{2}$

(E) $35\sqrt{3}$

(C) $12 + 7\sqrt{3}$

45. A function is defined as $f(x) = x^2 + 2$. What is the numerical value of $3f(0) + f(-1)f(2)$?

(A) 6

(D) 4

(B) 24

(E) 36

(C) 18

46. The first three terms of a progression are 3, 6, 12, ... What is the value of the tenth term?

(A) 1,200

(D) 1,536

(B) 2,468

(E) 3,272

(C) 188

47. Cube A has an edge 5m and a density of 2 kg/m³. Cube B has an edge of 2m and a density of 25 kg/m³. What is the ratio of their masses?

(A) $\dfrac{7}{8}$

(D) $\dfrac{5}{4}$

(B) $\dfrac{3}{4}$

(E) $\dfrac{9}{8}$

(C) $\dfrac{5}{3}$

Problems 48 and 49 pertain to the following figure of an open cube with a pyramid on top.

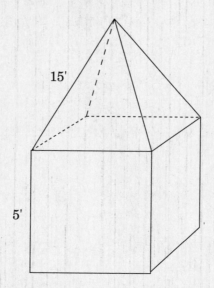

48. What is the surface area of the figure?

   (A) 272.9 square feet

   (B) 150.0 square feet

   (C) 247.9 square feet

   (D) 297.9 square feet

   (E) 194.11 square feet

49. What is the volume of the figure?

   (A) 272.9 cubic feet

   (B) 225.24 cubic feet

   (C) 248.24 cubic feet

   (D) 246.48 cubic feet

   (E) 135.24 cubic feet

50. An even function is a function that satisfies the condition $f(x) = f(-x)$. Which of the following is an even function?

   (A) $f(x) = \sin x$

   (B) $f(x) = x$

   (C) $f(x) = |\sin x| + 5$

   (D) $f(x) = |x^2 + x|$

   (E) $f(x) = x^3 - 1$

TEST 2

ANSWER KEY

1. (A)	14. (C)	27. (E)	40. (D)
2. (E)	15. (C)	28. (D)	41. (E)
3. (D)	16. (D)	29. (B)	42. (B)
4. (E)	17. (E)	30. (C)	43. (C)
5. (D)	18. (D)	31. (C)	44. (A)
6. (A)	19. (E)	32. (C)	45. (B)
7. (D)	20. (A)	33. (E)	46. (D)
8. (A)	21. (A)	34. (B)	47. (D)
9. (C)	22. (C)	35. (E)	48. (C)
10. (B)	23. (B)	36. (D)	49. (D)
11. (D)	24. (B)	37. (D)	50. (C)
12. (A)	25. (A)	38. (A)	
13. (D)	26. (A)	39. (B)	

DETAILED EXPLANATIONS
OF ANSWERS

1.　　**(A)**

There are four possible aces in a deck of 52 cards.

Calculator:

$$4 \boxed{\div} \ 52 \ \boxed{=} \ 0.0769$$

2.　　**(E)**

To solve we must factor both numerator and denominator of the given expression to lowest terms.

Expression: $\dfrac{a^2 - 3ab + 2b^2}{2b^2 + ab - a^2}$

Factoring the numerator:

$$a^2 - 3ab + 2ab^2 = (a - 2b)(a - b)$$

Factoring the denominator:

$$2b^2 + ab - a^2 = (2b - a)(b + a)$$

Rewriting the expression:

$$\frac{(a - 2b)(a - b)}{(2b - a)(b + a)} = \frac{a - 2b}{2b - a} \times \frac{a - b}{b + a}$$

We note that $a - 2b = -1(2b - a)$. Therefore,

$$\frac{a - 2b}{2b - a} = -1 \ .$$

The expression reduces to

$$-1\left[\frac{a - b}{b + a}\right] = \frac{b - a}{b + a} \ .$$

3.　　**(D)**

When given an inequality with an absolute value, recall the definition of absolute value:

$$|x| \equiv \begin{cases} x \text{ if } x \geq 0 \\ -x \text{ if } x < 0 \end{cases}$$

$$6x - 5 \leq 8 \text{ if } 6x - 5 \geq 0.$$

$$-6x + 5 \leq 8 \text{ if } 6x - 5 < 0.$$

$-6x + 5 \leq 8$ can be written as $6x - 5 \geq -8$.

We can set up both of these equations as follows:

$$-8 \leq 6x - 5 \leq 8$$

adding 5: $\quad -3 \leq 6x \leq 13$

dividing by 6: $\quad -\dfrac{1}{2} \leq x \leq \dfrac{13}{6}$.

So the values of x which satisfy $|\, 6x - 5 \,| \leq 8$ are $[-\dfrac{1}{2}, \dfrac{13}{6}]$.

4. **(E)**

The equation for the area of a rhombus is $\dfrac{1}{2}(D_1)(D_2)$.

Calculator:

$0.5 \boxed{\times} 12 \boxed{\times} 18 \boxed{=} 108$ square units.

5. **(D)**

Since $\overline{RS}$ is tangent to both circles, they meet the circles at right angles, and since Z is the midpoint, $\overline{RZ}$ and $\overline{ZS}$ are both 12 (with $\overline{XR}$ and $\overline{YS}$ both 5); so by the Pythagorean theorem, $\overline{XZ}$ and $\overline{YZ}$ are each 13.

Calculator:

$5 \boxed{x^2} \boxed{+} 12 \boxed{x^2} \boxed{=} \boxed{\sqrt{\ }} 13$.

Therefore, $\overline{XY} = 26$.

6. **(A)**

The first thing we do is draw a sketch on the coordinate axes:

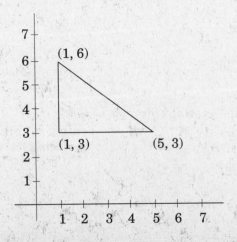

We see that the endpoints of the hypotenuse are (1, 6) and (5, 3). The slope is defined as:

$$m = \frac{y_2 - y_1}{x_2 - x_1}$$

$$m = \frac{3 - 6}{5 - 1} = \frac{-3}{4}$$

7.   **(D)**

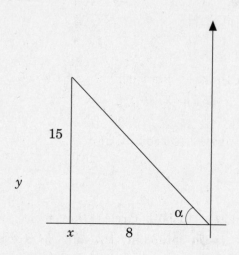

$$\sin \theta = \frac{\text{opp}}{\text{hyp}}; \quad \text{so} \quad \text{hyp} = \frac{\text{opp}}{\sin \theta}$$

Calculator:

3000 $\boxed{\div}$ 25 $\boxed{\sin}$ $\boxed{=}$ 7098.6 feet

8.   **(A)**

Calculator:

6.6726 $\boxed{\text{EE}}$ 11 $\boxed{+/-}$ $\boxed{\times}$ 5.98 $\boxed{\text{EE}}$ 24 $\boxed{\times}$ 7.36 $\boxed{\text{EE}}$ 22 $\boxed{=}$ $\boxed{\div}$ 3.84

$\boxed{\text{EE}}$ 8 $\boxed{x^2}$ $\boxed{=}$ 1.99 × 10^{20}

9.   **(C)**

When we arrange a certain number of objects, taken a certain number of times, in every possible way, we are dealing with permutations. One permutation is an arrangement of r objects selected from n objects.

The applicable formula is:

$$P(n, r) = \frac{n!}{(n-r)!}$$

where $n!$ stands for n factorial and is defined as $n \times (n-1) \times (n-2) \times \dots \times 1$. The letters a, b, c, d are 4 "objects." We are arranging them while taking them 3 at a time, e.g., abc, cda, etc. Therefore, we solve

$$P(4, 3) = \frac{4!}{(4-3)!} = \frac{4!}{1!} = \frac{4 \times 3 \times 2 \times 1}{1} = 24 \text{ arrangements.}$$

10.   **(B)**

   Calculator:

   25 ⊠ 15 ⊟ $\boxed{x^2}$ $\boxed{\log}$ ⊞ $\boxed{()}$ 25 $\boxed{\log}$ ⊞ 15 $\boxed{\log}$ $\boxed{()}$ ⊟ 2

11.   **(D)**

   The man originally buys the book for $20. He wishes to make a 50% profit on the book. To do this, he must sell the book for:

   $$20 + (50\%)(20) = \$30$$

He would like the $30 price to appear as if it is a mark down from an even higher price. We must find this phony price. Let this price be p. Then:

$$p - (40\%)(p) = 30$$

$$(0.60)p = 30$$

   Calculator:

   $$30 \div .6 = 50$$

   $$p = \$50$$

12.   **(A)**

   This problem illustrates the manipulation of complex numbers. First evaluate $(a + bi)^2$.

   $$(a + bi)^2 = (a + bi)(a + bi) = a^2 + abi + abi + b^2i^2$$

since $i^2 = -1$, $(a + bi)^2 = a^2 - b^2 + 2abi$

   Next evaluate $(a - bi)^2$:

   $$(a - bi)^2 = (a - bi)(a - bi) = a^2 - abi - abi + b^2i^2$$

This is equivalent to: $a^2 - b^2 - 2abi$.

   When subtracting complex numbers, we subtract the two real parts and the two imaginary parts separately. So,

   $$(a + bi)^2 - (a - bi)^2 = [(a^2 - b^2) + 2abi] - [(a^2 - b^2) - 2abi]$$

$a^2 - b^2$ disappears and we are left with:

$$2abi - (-2abi) = 4abi$$

13. **(D)**

First we draw a sketch of the problem:

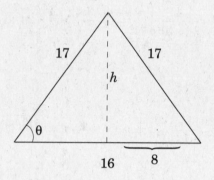

Let the base angle $= \theta$. We need $\tan\theta$. In the sketch, this is $\dfrac{h}{8}$. To get h, the Pythagorean theorem is invoked:

$$a^2 + b^2 = c^2$$

In the sketch, this comes to:

$$h^2 + 8^2 = 17^2$$

Solving for h: $h^2 = 17^2 - 8^2$

$$h = \sqrt{17^2 - 8^2} = 15$$

$$\tan\theta = \frac{h}{8} = \frac{15}{8}$$

14. **(C)**

$$A_r - 15(A_c) = l \times w - 15(\pi r^2) \qquad r^2 = \frac{\text{diameter}}{2}$$

Calculator:

$$10 \;\boxed{\times}\; 16 \;\boxed{-}\; 15 \;\boxed{\times}\; \boxed{\pi} \;\boxed{\times}\; 1.5 \;\boxed{x^2}\; \boxed{=} \; 53.97 \approx 54$$

15. **(C)**

The area of a square is the square of its side. When the diagonal is known, the side can be found by the relation:

$$2s^2 = d^2 \qquad \text{(by Pythagorean theorem)}$$

or
$$s^2 = \frac{d^2}{2}$$

Since $A = s^2$, we can say: $A = \frac{d^2}{2}$.

The length of the diagonal d is found by the distance formula:

$$d = \sqrt{(x_2 - y_1)^2 + (y_2 - y_1)^2}$$

Substituting the two endpoints:

$$d = \sqrt{(3 - (-1))^2 + (8 - 2)^2} = \sqrt{(4)^2 + (6)^2}$$

$$d = \sqrt{16 + 36} = \sqrt{52}$$

Squaring: $d^2 = 52$

Solving for the area: $A = \frac{d^2}{2} = \frac{52}{2} = 26$

16.   **(D)**

This is a function of a function. Substituting the value for A and B gives:

$$(5 * 4) = (5 - 4)\,(5 + 4)$$
$$= (1)\,(9)$$
$$= 9$$

then $(6 * 9) = (6 - 9)\,(6 + 9)$
$$= (-3)\,(15)$$
$$= -45$$

or: $(A - B)\,(A + B) = A^2 - B^2$

This becomes

$$6^2 - (5^2 - 4^2)^2$$

Calculator:

6 $\boxed{x^2}$ $\boxed{-}$ $\boxed{()}$ 5 $\boxed{x^2}$ $\boxed{-}$ 4 $\boxed{x^2}$ $\boxed{()}$ $\boxed{x^2}$ $\boxed{=}$ -45

17.   **(E)**

Since the absolute value of an expression is non-negative, it must be greater than -1. Therefore, the solution set is the entire real axis which contains infinite number of integers.

18.   **(D)**

This problem is solved by the procedure of polynomial long division:

$$\begin{array}{r} x^2 + 9x + 42 \\ x-5\overline{)x^3 + 4x^2 - 3x + 8} \end{array}$$

Multiply $x - 5$ by x^2.

$$\frac{-(x^3 - 5x^2)}{9x^2 - 3x}$$

Multiply $x - 5$ by $9x^2$.

$$\frac{-(9x^3 - 45x)}{42x + 8}$$

Multiply $x - 5$ by 42.

$$\frac{-(42x - 210)}{218}$$

Thus, the remainder is 218.

19.   **(E)**

The fraction is a complex fraction. To simplify, we must multiply both numerator and denominator by $b^2 - 2b$:

$$\frac{\dfrac{2}{b^2 a^2}}{\dfrac{1}{b^2 - 2b}} \times \frac{b^2 - 2b}{b^2 - 2b} = \frac{2(b^2 - 2b)}{a^2 b^2}$$

Multiplying through in the numerator:

$$\frac{2b^2 - 4b}{a^2 b^2}$$

The numerator is factored and like terms are cancelled.

$$\frac{(2b - 4)b}{a^2 b^2} = \frac{2b - 4}{a^2 b}$$

20.   **(A)**

To find the other root of the quadratic equation, we must first solve for the coefficient a.

Substituting 6 for x, we obtain:

$$x^2 - ax + 12 = 0$$
$$6^2 - a(6) + 12 = 0$$

$$36 + 12 = 6a$$
$$48 = 6a$$
$$8 = a .$$

The quadratic equation that we obtain is:

$$x^2 - 8x + 12 = 0$$

Factoring: $(x - 6)(x - 2) = 0$,

therefore, the roots are 6 and 2.

21.   **(A)**

Two angles that are complementary must have measures that add up to 90°.

Let the angle equal x, its complement equal $x - 40$. These angles must add up to 90°. Therefore,

$$x + x - 40 = 90$$
$$2x = 130$$
$$x = 65°$$

Therefore, the angle is 65°.

22.   **(C)**

The angles of a triangle must add up to 180°. Following this theorem with the angles given:

$$(x) + (y) + (x + y) = 180°$$

Adding like terms:

$$2x + 2y = 180°$$

Dividing the equation by 2:

$$x + y = 90°$$

$x + y$ is an angle that is given. Since it equals to 90°, the triangle that contains it must be a right triangle.

23.   **(B)**

As a rule, the intersection between two planes is a line. We must find the two planes of which A and G are simultaneous members. One is given as plane DAF. From inspection, the other plane is plane ABG. All points on AG are simultaneously in the planes DAF and ABG. Note also that plane GFA is plane DAF and thus their intersection would not be a line, but rather the plane itself. Therefore, the only correct response would be plane ABG.

24.   **(B)**

Note that the distance from A to the center is equivalent to the distance from the center to B. Also note that to get from point A, $(-2, 1)$, to the center, $(3, 4)$, the movement would be 5 units to the right and 3 units upward. Therefore, starting at the center, $(3, 4)$, and similarly moving +5 units on the x-axis and +3 units on the y-axis, we would arrive at point $(8, 7)$ which must be B, since this movement maintains the slope.

25.   **(A)**

The equation given is

$$\cos 2x + 3\sin^2 x - 6\sin x + 4 = 0 \ .$$

The identity for $\cos 2x$ is implemented:

$$\cos 2x = 1 - 2\sin^2 x \tag{1}$$

Substituting in equation (1) for $\cos 2x$:

$$1 - 2\sin^2 x + 3\sin^2 x - 6\sin x + 4 = 0$$

Simplifying: $\sin^2 x - 6\sin x + 5 = 0$

Factoring: $(\sin x - 5)(\sin x - 1) = 0$

The two equations that are set up are:

$$\sin x - 5 = 0 \Rightarrow \sin x = 5 \tag{2}$$

$$\sin x - 1 = 0 \Rightarrow \sin x = 1 \tag{3}$$

Equation (2) has no solution because the function $\sin x$ takes on a maximum value of 1. That leaves equation (3). Solving:

$$\sin x = 1$$

$$\sin^{-1}(\sin x) = \sin^{-1} 1$$

$$x = \sin^{-1} 1 \ .$$

The angles which have sin1 are

$$\frac{\pi}{2}, \frac{5\pi}{2}, \frac{9\pi}{2}, \ \dots$$

in other words, $2n\pi + \dfrac{\pi}{2}$ where $n = 0, 1, 2, 3, \ \dots$. Thus the solution set is

$\{x = 2n\pi + \dfrac{\pi}{2}\}$.

26.   **(A)**

This is an example of a composite function. First we must evaluate $f(6)$. From the figure, we see that $f(6) = 2$. Thus $f(f(6)) = f(2)$. From the figure, $f(2) = -2$, so that $f(f(6)) = -2$.

27.   **(E)**

Since the equation is set up for Celsius, you must transpose the equation to $C = \dfrac{5}{9}(F - 32)$.

Calculator:

5 ÷ 9 × ( ) 165 − 32 ( ) = 73.9°

28.   **(D)**

This problem is solved most easily by recognizing that the maximum rectangular area is contained by a square. We are given the perimeter.

$$P = 800$$

Since a square has 4 equal sides, each side is:

$$s = \frac{P}{4} = \frac{800}{4} = 200 \ .$$

The area of a square is s^2.

Therefore, the maximum rectangular area is

$$s^2 = 200^2$$

$$= 40,000 \ \text{ft}^2$$

29.   **(B)**

To solve, the inverse of the logarithmic function must be used. This is stated as:

$$y = \log_a N$$
$$N = a^y$$

Applying this to the given equation yields $N = 8^{\frac{2}{3}}$. So

$$N = \sqrt[3]{8^2} = \sqrt[3]{64} = 4$$

30.   **(C)**

We seek all the numbers that satisfy the equation,

$$27^{x^{2+1}} = 243 \ .$$

The best way to solve this problem is to take logarithms to the base 3 on both sides. After this, we obtain:

$$\log_3 27^{x^{2+1}} = \log_3 243$$

Since $\log_b x^r = r \log_b x$, we obtain:

$$(x^2 + 1)\,(\log_3 27) = \log_3 243$$

Since $27 = 3^3$, $\log_3 27 = 3$.

Similarly, $243 = 3^5$ and $\log_3 243 = 5$. Thus, the equation becomes:

$$3(x^2 + 1) = 5$$

Solving for x:

$$x^2 + 1 = \frac{5}{3}$$

Subtracting 1 from both sides:

$$x^2 = \frac{2}{3}$$

Taking square roots:

$$x = \pm\sqrt{\frac{2}{3}}$$

Thus, one solution is

$$-\sqrt{\frac{2}{3}}$$

31.   **(C)**

Since the solutions of the system, x and y, are given, these values can be substituted into the two equations and the unknown coefficients are solved for.

Substituting $x = 2$ and $y = 1$:

$$2a + b = 20 \tag{1}$$

$$2b + a = 16 \tag{2}$$

We can solve for b by using equation (1),

$$b = 20 - 2a\ .$$

Substituting this into equation (2) yields

$$2(20 - 2a) + a = 16.$$

Simplifying:

$$40 - 4a + a = 16$$

$$40 - 3a = 16$$

$$-3a = -4$$

$$3a = -24$$

$$a = 8$$

Substituting 8 for a in equation (1) we obtain:

$$2(8) + b = 20$$

$$16 + b = 20$$

$$b = 4$$

Thus, $a = 8$, $b = 4$.

32.   **(C)**

If a figure has exterior angles that are equal, then the figure is a form of a regular polygon.

From a theorem, the number of sides of a regular polygon can be found from the measure of an exterior angle. The relation is:

$$\text{exterior angle} = \frac{360°}{n},$$

where n is the number of sides. Solving for n:

$$n = \frac{360°}{\text{exterior angle}}$$

Substituting 72° for exterior angle:

$$n = \frac{360°}{72°} = 5$$

A five-sided figure is a pentagon.

33.   **(E)**

Drawing a diagram will help clarify:

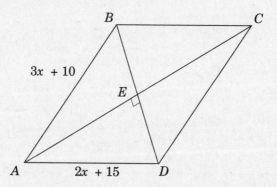

where $\angle BAD = 12x$, BD = the shorter diagonal, and AC = the longer diagonal.

Since all sides of a rhombus are equal:

$$3x + 10 = 2x + 15$$

Solving for x:

$$x = 5$$

Substituting to find $\angle BAD$:

$$\angle BAD = 12(5) = 60$$

In a rhombus the diagonals bisect the angles they are drawn to, thus

$$\angle EAD = \frac{1}{2}(\angle BAD) = \frac{1}{2}60 = 30$$

Side $AD = 2x + 15 = 2(5) + 15 = 10 + 15 = 25$

This is the hypotenuse of a 30-60 right triangle AED. To get segment ED, we use $\angle EAD$:

$$\sin EAD = \frac{ED}{AD}.$$

$$ED = (\sin EAD)AD = (\sin 30)25 = \frac{25}{2}$$

Since the diagonals of the rhombus bisect each other $ED = BE$. Thus,

$$BD = ED + BE = \frac{25}{2} + \frac{25}{2} = 25.$$

34.　　**(B)**

Break the graph down into triangles and rectangles whose area we can find.

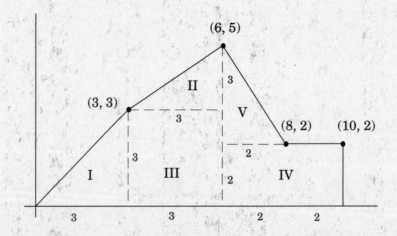

$$\text{Area} = I + II + III + IV + V$$

$$= \frac{1}{2}(b)(h) + \frac{1}{2}(b)(h) + (l)(w) + (l)(w) + \frac{1}{2}(b)(h)$$

$$= (0.5)(3)(3) + (0.5)(3)(2) + (3)(3) + (2)(4) + (0.5)(3)(2)$$

Calculator:

.5 $\boxed{\times}$ 3 $\boxed{\times}$ 3 $\boxed{+}$ .5 $\boxed{\times}$ 3 $\boxed{\times}$ 2 $\boxed{+}$ 3 $\boxed{\times}$ 3 $\boxed{+}$ 2 $\boxed{\times}$ 4 $\boxed{+}$ .5 $\boxed{\times}$ 3 $\boxed{\times}$ 2

$\boxed{=}$ 27.5

35.   **(E)**

The absolute value function is used. In the function $f(x) = |x|$, for every x value $f(x)$ is the positive magnitude of that value. Thus, the sketch of $f(x) = |\sin x|$ is given by:

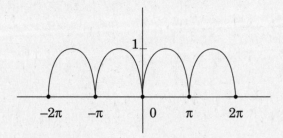

The negative of this is $f(x) = -|\sin x|$. This is simply the sketch of $|\sin x|$ inverted:

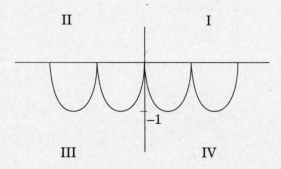

This graph lies only in quadrants III and IV.

36.   **(D)**

$$\text{Soda} + \text{Bottle} = 50 \qquad \text{(equation 1)}$$

and $\qquad \text{Soda} = \text{Bottle} + 30 \qquad \text{(equation 2)}$

so by substituting equation 2 into equation 1

$$(\text{Bottle} + 30) + \text{Bottle} = 50$$

$$2\text{Bottle} = 50 - 30$$
$$\text{Bottle} = 10$$

$$50 - 30 \div 2 = 10$$

37.   **(D)**

To solve $7 + 2x$, we must first solve for x. We use the equation $7x = \dfrac{3}{5}x$.

Subtracting $\dfrac{3}{5}x$ from both sides we obtain

$$\frac{32}{5}x = 0 \ ,$$

from which we see

$$x = 0 \ .$$

Substituting:

$$7 + 2x = 7 + 2(0) = 7$$

38.   **(A)**

To solve this quadratic equation, we invoke the quadratic formula:

$$x = \frac{-b \pm \sqrt{b^2 - 4ac}}{2a}$$

The equation is $x^2 + 2x + 7 = 0$. So $a = 1$, $b = 2$, and $c = 7$.

Substituting into the formula:

$$x = \frac{-2 \pm \sqrt{2^2 - 4\,(1)\,(7)}}{2\,(1)}$$

$$= \frac{-2 \pm \sqrt{4 - 28}}{2} = -1 \pm \sqrt{-6}$$

Since $i = \sqrt{-1}$, $\ x = -1 \pm i\sqrt{6}$.

These roots are complex conjugates of each other.

39.   **(B)**

The problem may best be solved by setting up a system of simultaneous equations. Since there are two unknowns, namely the units digit and the tens digit, two equations are needed to solve for these variables, u and t, respectively.

One equation can be obtained from the fact that the sum of the digits is 9. Thus

$$t + u = 9 . \tag{1}$$

The other condition states that the number itself (which can be expressed as $10t + 1u$ since the number has t tens and u units) is equal to 9 times the units digit. Therefore, we obtain:

$$10t + u = 9u . \tag{2}$$

Solving equation (1) for t, we have $t = 9 - u$. Now substituting this value of t into equation (2), we obtain:

$$9u = 10(9 - u) + u .$$

Simplifying we obtain:

$$9u = 90 - 10u + u$$

$$9u = 90 - 9u$$

$$18u = 90$$

$$u = \frac{90}{18}$$

$$u = 5$$

Substituting this value of u into equation (1) we obtain 4 as the value of t, therefore the required number is 45.

40. **(D)**

Since the vertices of the square bisect the sides of the triangle, the two sides are 4 units, making the hypotenuse $4\sqrt{2}$; so it is an isosceles triangle and the area $= \frac{1}{2}bh.$

$$.5 \times 4 \times 4 = 8$$

41. **(E)**

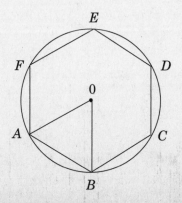

In order to find the area of the given circle, we need to know how large its radius is, so that we could employ the formula for the area of a circle, which is $A = \pi r^2$.

Recall that since $ABCDEF$ is a regular hexagon, the measure of the central angle $AOB = \dfrac{360°}{6} = 60°$. Since $\overline{AO} \cong \overline{BO}$, $\angle OAB = \angle OBA$, but since the points O, A, and B describe a triangle, and the sum of the interior angles of a triangle must add up to $180°$,

$$180° = \angle AOB + \angle OAB + \angle OBA \,.$$

Substituting the fact that $\angle AOB = 60°$ and $\angle OAB = \angle OBA$, we obtain:

$$180° = 60° + 2\angle OAB \qquad \text{or}$$
$$120° = 2\angle OAB \qquad \text{or}$$
$$60° = \angle OAB$$

So now we know that $\angle OAB = 60°$ and therefore $\angle OBA = 60°$. Therefore, all three angles are $60°$. So $\triangle AOB$ is equiangular and therefore equilateral. Since $\overline{AB} = 7$, $\overline{AO} = 7$, this is the radius of the given circle.

Recall $A = \pi r^2$, with $r = 7$ we find that the area of the circle is equal to 49π.

42.　　**(B)**

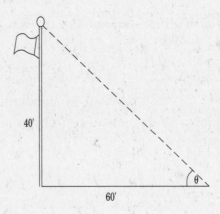

$$\tan\theta = \frac{\text{opp}}{\text{adj}} \Rightarrow \theta = \tan^{-1}\!\left(\frac{\text{opp}}{\text{adj}}\right)$$

Calculator:

40 $\boxed{\div}$ 60 $\boxed{=}$ $\boxed{\text{inv}}$ $\boxed{\text{tan}}$ 33.7

43.   **(C)**

The simplest way to solve this is to get the equation into slope intercept form:

$$y = mx + b \ ,$$

where m is the slope and b is the y-intercept. The given equation is:

$$x = 3y + 8$$

Subtracting 8 from both sides:

$$3y = x - 8$$

Dividing by 3:

$$y = \frac{1}{3}x - \frac{8}{3}$$

From this and the slope intercept form, $b = \dfrac{-8}{3}$. Thus, the y-intercept is

$\dfrac{-8}{3}$.

44.   **(A)**

To solve, the law of tangents is applied to sides x and y and angles B and C. So applied, the relation we use is:

$$\frac{x - y}{x + y} = \frac{\tan\dfrac{1}{2}(B - C)}{\tan\dfrac{1}{2}(B + C)}$$

Angle B is 105, angle C is 15, so

$$\frac{1}{2}(B - C) = \frac{1}{2}(105 - 15) = \frac{1}{2}(90) = 45$$

and $\tan 45 = 1$.

Also, $\dfrac{1}{2}(B + C) = \dfrac{1}{2}(105 + 15) = \dfrac{1}{2}(120) = 60$

and $\tan 60 = \sqrt{3}$.

Since y is 10 less than x, $x - y = 10$. We use equation (1) to solve for $x + y$.

Substituting values:

$$\frac{10}{x + y} = \frac{1}{\sqrt{3}} \ ,$$

and cross multiplying:

$$x + y = 10\sqrt{3} \ .$$

This gives us two equations and two unknowns which allows us to solve for x.

$$x - y = 10$$

$$x + y = 10\sqrt{3}$$

Adding the two equations we obtain:

$$2x = 10 + 10\sqrt{3}$$

Dividing by two, our result is:

$$x = 5 + 5\sqrt{3} \ .$$

45.   **(B)**

We are given $f(x) = x^2 + 2$. We must find $f(0)$, $f(-1)$, and $f(2)$.

Replacing x with zero we obtain:

$$f(0) = 0^2 + 2 = 2$$

Similarly:

$$f(-1) = (-1)^2 + 2 = 3$$

Finally:

$$f(2) = (2)^2 + 2 = 6$$

Evaluating:

$$3f(0) + f(-1)f(2)$$
$$= 3(2) + (3)\,(6)$$
$$= 6 + 18 = 24$$

46.   **(D)**

The progression given is a geometric progression. The expression for the nth term of a geometric progression is:

$$1_n = a_1 r^{n-1}$$

where a_1 is the first term and r is the common ratio between terms.

In the given sequence, the first term is 3. The common ratio is found to be $\dfrac{6}{3} = \dfrac{12}{6} = 2$.

Therefore, letting $n = 10$ (for the tenth term), we have:

$$1_{10} = 3(2)^{10-1} = 3(2)^9 \ .$$

Since $2^9 = 512$:

$$1_{10} = 3(512) = 1{,}536$$

47. **(D)**

The edges of cubes A and B are given:

Edge $A = 5$m,

Edge $B = 2$m .

Their densities are also given:

Density $A = 2$ kg/m^3 ,

Density $B = 25$ kg/m^3 .

The mass of an object equals its volume multiplied by its density. That is:

Mass = Volume $\times$ Density

From this:

Mass A = Volume $A \times$ Density A and $\qquad\qquad$ (1)

Mass B = Volume $B \times$ Density B

The volume of a cube is the cube of its edge: s^3. Therefore,

Volume A = (Edge A)^3 = $(5$m$)^3$ = 125m^3 ,

Volume B = (Edge B)^3 = $(2$m$)^3$ = 8m^3 .

We may now find the masses of the cubes. Substituting for volume and density in equations (1), we obtain:

Mass A = $(125$m$^3)$ $(2$ kg/m$^3)$ = 250 kg

Mass B = $(8$m$^3)$ $(25$ kg/m$^3)$ = 200 kg

The ratio $\dfrac{\text{Mass } A}{\text{Mass } B}$ is seen to be $\dfrac{250 \text{ kg}}{200 \text{ kg}} = \dfrac{5}{4}$.

48. **(C)**

To find the area of the pyramid, find the area of each triangle.

$$A = \frac{1}{2}bh$$

The base is $\dfrac{1}{2}$ the length of the side of the cube, $b = \dfrac{1}{2}(5) = 2.5$. The height is found by the Pythagorean theorem, $a^2 + b^2 = c^2$.

$$h^2 + 2.5^2 = 15^2$$

$$h = \sqrt{15^2 - 2.5^2}$$

Calculator:

15 $\boxed{x^2}$ $\boxed{-}$ 2.5 $\boxed{x^2}$ $\boxed{=}$ $\boxed{\sqrt{}}$ 14.79

Use calculator to find surface area of pyramid.

Calculator:

4 $\boxed{\times}$ .5 $\boxed{\times}$ 5 $\boxed{\times}$ 14.79 $\boxed{=}$ 147.9

Use calculator to find surface area of the open cube:

$5^2 + 5^2 + 5^2 + 5^2 = 100$

Total surface area = 247.9

49.   **(D)**

To find the pyramid's height, use the Pythagorean theorem on the triangle:

$$a^2 + b^2 = c^2$$

$$h^2 + \left(\frac{5}{2}\sqrt{2}\right)^2 = 15^2$$

$$h = \sqrt{15^2 - \left(\frac{5}{2}\sqrt{2}\right)^2}$$

Calculator:

15 $\boxed{x^2}$ $\boxed{-}$ $\boxed{(\ )}$ $\frac{5}{2}$ $\boxed{x^2}$ $\boxed{\times}$ 2 $\boxed{(\ )}$ $\boxed{=}$ $\boxed{\sqrt{}}$ 14.57738

Pyramid's volume + cube's volume = total volume

$$\frac{1}{3}bh + 5^3 = \text{total volume}$$

Calculator:

1 $\boxed{\div}$ 3 $\boxed{\times}$ 5 $\boxed{\times}$ 5 $\boxed{\times}$ 14.57738 $\boxed{+}$ 5 $\boxed{y^x}$ 3 $\boxed{=}$ 246.48

50.   **(C)**

The definition of an even function, as given, means that the function $f(x)$ takes on equal values for both positive and negative x. The function $\sin x$ does not follow this condition. However, the function $|\sin x|$ does. This can be verified by sketching the graph of $|\sin x|$.

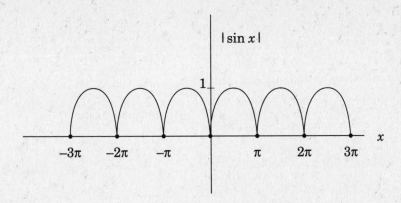

Every value of $f(x)$ has a corresponding equal value of $f(-x)$. Adding 5 to this function just raises the entire function by 5. Thus, the function $f(x) = |\sin x| + 5$ is an even function. Now note that although the function given as $f(x) = |x^2 + x|$ employs the absolute value function, $f(3) \neq f(-3)$.

THE SAT SUBJECT TEST IN

Math
Level 1

PRACTICE TEST 3

SAT Mathematics
Level 1

Practice Test 3

Time: 1 Hour
50 Questions

DIRECTIONS: Choose the best answer for each question and mark the letter of your selection on the corresponding answer sheet.

NOTES:

(1) Some questions require the use of a calculator. You must decide when the use of your calculator will be helpful.

(2) Make sure your calculator is in degree mode.

(3) All figures are drawn to scale and lie in a plane unless otherwise stated.

(4) The domain of any function f is the set of all real numbers x for which $f(x)$ is a real number, unless other information is provided.

REFERENCE INFORMATION: The following information may be helpful in answering some of the questions.

Volume of a right circular cone with radius r and height h $\qquad V = \dfrac{1}{3}\pi r^2 h$

Lateral area of a right circular cone with circumference c and slant height l $\qquad S = \dfrac{1}{2}cl$

Volume of a sphere with radius r $\qquad V = \dfrac{4}{3}\pi r^3$

Surface area of a sphere with radius r $\qquad S = 4\pi r^2$

Volume of a pyramid with base area B and height h $\qquad V = \dfrac{1}{3}Bh$

1. Given the expression

$$z = \frac{(x+2a)\,(b-c)^2}{d^{\frac{1}{3}}},$$

if $x = 9$, $a = 3.5$, $b = 6$, $c = 10$, and $d = 8$, then z equals

(A) 182.00

(D) 128.00

(B) 12.80

(E) −128.00

(C) 10.67

2. Find the surface area of the solid below.

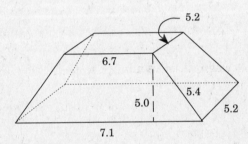

(A) 94.75

(D) 130.06

(B) 179.98

(E) 114.28

(C) 196.92

3. If the cost of 12 chickens is $17.40, and if the cost of a chicken and a duck together is $3.40, what is the cost of a duck?

(A) $1.45

(D) $1.95

(B) $1.65

(E) $2.10

(C) $1.80

4. $A = (x^2 + 3xy + 2y^2)\,(7xy - y^3)$

If $x = 1.25$ and $y = 2.75$, find the value for A.

(A) 88.17

(D) −19.67

(B) 6,288.82

(E) 8.28

(C) 88.03

5. In the figure below, if B bisects the segment AD, then the length of segment CD is

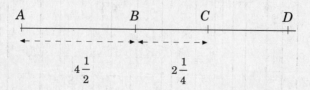

(A) $1\dfrac{3}{4}$.

(D) $2\dfrac{3}{4}$.

(B) $2\dfrac{1}{4}$.

(E) $3\dfrac{1}{2}$.

(C) $2\dfrac{1}{2}$.

6. What is the distance between $(0, -2)$ and $(7, 0)$?

(A) $\sqrt{43}$

(D) $\sqrt{53}$

(B) $\sqrt{45}$

(E) $\sqrt{55}$

(C) $\sqrt{47}$

7. The area of triangle DEF is

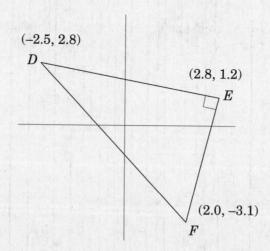

(A) 12.1 .

(D) 15.6 .

(B) 24.2 .

(E) 18.3 .

(C) 10.2 .

8. If $5 < a < 8$ and $6 < b < 9$, then

    (A) $45 < ab < 48$.

    (B) $30 < ab < 45$.

    (C) $30 < ab < 72$.

    (D) $54 < ab < 72$.

    (E) $5 < ab < 72$.

9. In the figure below, two lines AB and CD intersect at E, making the angles shown. What is the value of $x + y$?

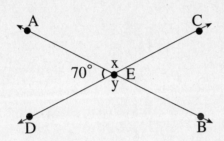

    (A) 140°

    (B) 165°

    (C) 180°

    (D) 200°

    (E) 220°

10. If $\dfrac{a}{b} = 4$, then what is $a^2 - 16b^2$?

    (A) −16

    (B) −4

    (C) 0

    (D) 4

    (E) 16

11. Given the linear equations:

    $$5x - 3y = 16$$

    $$2x + 7y = 12$$

    The solution (x, y) is:

    (A) (3.610, 0.683)

    (B) (0.262, 0.976)

    (C) (3.814, 0.976)

    (D) (3.610, 0.976)

    (E) (0.976, 3.814)

12. If $\dfrac{\frac{1}{b}}{\frac{1}{3}} = \dfrac{1}{4}$, then $b =$

    (A) $\dfrac{1}{4}$.

    (D) $\dfrac{4}{3}$.

    (B) $\dfrac{3}{4}$.

    (E) 12.

    (C) $\dfrac{13}{4}$.

13. $\sqrt{8} + 3\sqrt{18} - 7\sqrt{2} =$

    (A) $3 - 3\sqrt{2}$

    (D) $4\sqrt{2}$

    (B) 0

    (E) $10\sqrt{2}$

    (C) $6\sqrt{2} - 4\sqrt{3}$

14. In the figure shown, line r is parallel to line l. Find the measure of angle RBC.

    (A) 30°

    (D) 100°

    (B) 80°

    (E) 110°

    (C) 90°

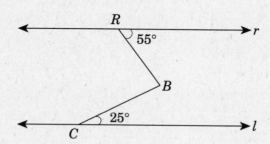

15. The solution to the pair of equations

$$\begin{cases} ax + by = 8 \\ bx + ay = 10 \end{cases}$$

is $x = 2$, $y = 1$. Find a and b.

(A) $a = 3$, $b = 4$

(D) $a = 2$, $b = 4$

(B) $a = 3$, $b = 3$

(E) $a = 4$, $b = 4$

(C) $a = 2$, $b = 3$

16. The distance between A and B is:

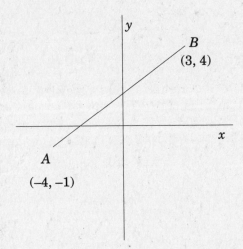

(A) 2.24

(D) −8.60

(B) 8.60

(E) −2.24

(C) 7.62

17. In the figure below, $\angle ABC$ measures $45°$. If $AB = AC = 3$ and $AF = CF = AD = BD$, then $BC =$

(A) $2\sqrt{2}$.

(D) $2\sqrt{3}$.

(B) $3\sqrt{2}$.

(E) $3\sqrt{3}$.

(C) 3.

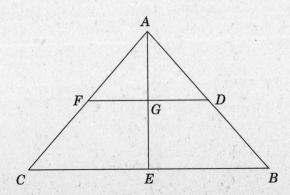

18. If $f(x) = 4.3x - 5.4$, what is $f^{-1}(9.2)$?

(A) 3.40

(D) 2.50

(B) 0.88

(E) 0.91

(C) 1.05

19. If $f(x) = x^5 - 3x^4 + 4x^2 - 6x + 7$, what is $f(3)$?

(A) 511

(D) 25

(B) 43

(E) 268

(C) 52

20. In the figure below, $\triangle ABC$ is a right-angled isosceles triangle. If AD = 7 and AB = 4, what is the area of $\triangle DCB$?

(A) 2

(D) 8

(B) 4

(E) 10

(C) 6

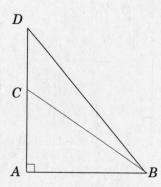

21. If $f(x) = \dfrac{2x-1}{x}$ and $g(x) = \dfrac{1}{3x}$, then $f(g(2)) =$

(A) −4

(D) 2

(B) −2

(E) 4

(C) 0

22. If $\sqrt[6]{x^2} = \sqrt[3]{b}$, what is x if $b = 25$?

   (A) 8.5

   (B) 25

   (C) 20

   (D) 16

   (E) 15

23. The polygons shown in the figure are similar. What is the length of k?

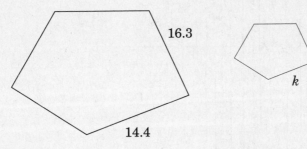

   (A) 2.83 .

   (B) 3.76 .

   (C) 3.53 .

   (D) 4.57 .

   (E) 3.45 .

24. If there exist positive integers a and b such that $8a + 12b = c$, then c must be divisible by

   (A) 3.

   (B) 4.

   (C) 18.

   (D) 24.

   (E) 96.

25. $(9.04)^{x-1} = (4.37)^x$. What is the value of x?

   (A) 0.3302

   (B) 0.9562

   (C) 0.6698

   (D) 3.0285

   (E) 1.5613

26. In the right-angled triangle ABC, if $\cos A = \dfrac{12}{13}$, then the length of BC is

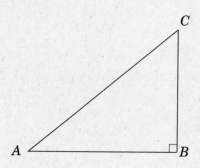

(A) 1.

(B) 5.

(C) $2\sqrt{5}$.

(D) $5\sqrt{3}$.

(E) 2.

27. Which of the following is the graph of a one-to-one function of x?

(A)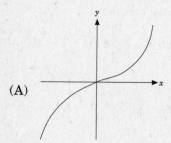

(B)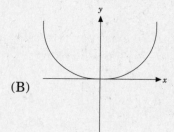

(C)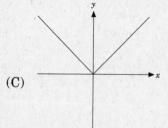

(D)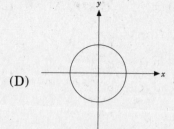

(E)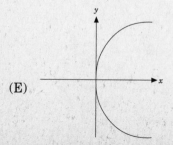

28. A sphere is inscribed in a cube whose edges are 20 cm long. What is the ratio of the volume of the sphere to the volume of the cube?

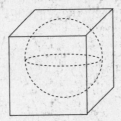

(A) 4.189

(B) 1.910

(C) 0.524

(D) 0.628

(E) 1.592

29. The area of circle D is:

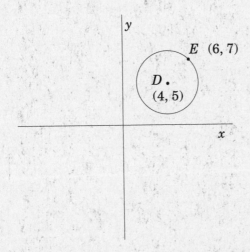

(A) 33.3 .

(B) 25.2 .

(C) 8.09 .

(D) 99.9 .

(E) 21.5 .

30. $\dfrac{b+3}{b^3-8} + \dfrac{b+2}{b^5-5} = \dfrac{b-3}{b^2-7}$

What values of b cannot be roots of the equation?

(A) 2.65, 2.00, 1.38

(D) 2.65, –2.00, 1.38

(B) 1.91, 2.00, 1.67

(E) 2.65, 2.00, 1.67

(C) –2.65, 2.00, –1.38

31. Given the mapping:

$$G:(x,\ y) \to \left(\dfrac{x^3}{5},\ \dfrac{xy-5x^2}{y} \right)$$

What is $G:(2,\ 4) \to (?,\ ?)$?

(A) (12.8, –36)

(D) (–36, 12.8)

(B) (–12.8, 36)

(E) (–3.0, 6.4)

(C) (1.6, –3)

32. If $\cos\beta = 0.5$, what is $\tan\alpha$?

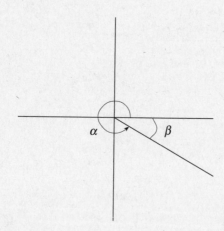

(A) 1.732

(D) –1.732

(B) 0.866

(E) –0.867

(C) 1.155

33. If $f(x) = 3x + 2$ and $g(f(x)) = x$, then $g(x) =$

(A) $\dfrac{x-2}{3}$.

(D) $3x - 2$.

(B) $\dfrac{x}{3} - 2$.

(E) $4x + 9$.

(C) $3x$.

34. In the figure, if $AC \mid \mid DF$ and if $DE = a$ and $EF = b$, then $\dfrac{AB}{AC} =$

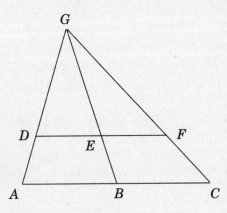

(A) $\dfrac{a}{b}$.

(D) $\dfrac{b}{a}$.

(B) $\dfrac{a}{a+b}$.

(E) $\dfrac{b}{a} - 1$.

(C) $\dfrac{a}{b} - 1$.

35. Solve for x.

$$2.4x^2 - 7.3x + 5.3 = 0$$

(A) 1.08, 6.97

(D) 3.69, 2.40

(B) 3.64, 0.60

(E) 1.84, 1.20

(C) −1.19, −1.84

36. In the figure, if *MNOP* is a square with *MN* = *x*, then the ratio

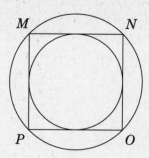

$$\frac{\text{circumference of circumscribed circle}}{\text{circumference of inscribed circle}} =$$

(A) 2

(B) $\sqrt{2}$

(C) $\dfrac{1}{\sqrt{2}}$

(D) $2\sqrt{2}$

(E) $\dfrac{1}{2}$

37. A straight line is formed by (1, 4) and (3, 2); find the *y*-intercept of the line.

(A) −1

(B) 2

(C) 3

(D) 5

(E) 7

38. If $\dfrac{1}{2x} = \dfrac{1}{\dfrac{1}{y}}$ and $1 < x < 5$, then which of the following is true?

(A) $0.1 < y < 0.5$

(B) $0.1 < y < 1$

(C) $1 < y < 5$

(D) $0.5 < y < 2$

(E) $0.5 < y < 5$

39. Given two spheres of the same kind of material, if the ratio of their radii is $\frac{2}{3}$, then what is the ratio of their weight?

(A) 1

(D) $\frac{4}{9}$

(B) $\frac{3}{2}$

(E) $\frac{8}{27}$

(C) $\frac{2}{3}$

40. In the right-angled triangle, c is equal to which of the following?

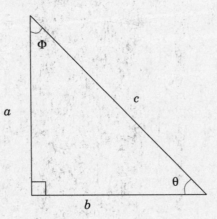

I. $\sqrt{a^2 + b^2}$

II. $\dfrac{b}{\cos\theta}$

III. $\dfrac{b}{\sin\Phi}$

(A) I only.

(D) I and III only.

(B) II only.

(E) I, II, and III.

(C) III only.

41. If the points $P(7, 0)$, $Q(0, -3)$, $R(0, 3)$, and $S(-7, 0)$ are connected to form a quadrilateral $PQRS$, the area of the quadrilateral will be

(A) 42.

(D) 84.

(B) 21.

(E) 49.

(C) 63.

42. What is the probability that in a single throw of two dice the sum of 10 will appear?

(A) $\dfrac{10}{36}$

(D) $\dfrac{2}{10}$

(B) $\dfrac{1}{6}$

(E) $\dfrac{11}{12}$

(C) $\dfrac{1}{12}$

43. If θ is an acute angle and $\cos\theta = \dfrac{a}{b}$, where $a > 0$, $b > 0$, and $a \neq b$, then $\sin\theta =$

(A) $\dfrac{\sqrt{a^2 - b^2}}{b}$.

(D) $\dfrac{\sqrt{b^2 - a^2}}{a}$.

(B) $\dfrac{\sqrt{b^2 - a^2}}{b}$.

(E) $\dfrac{b}{a}$.

(C) $\dfrac{\sqrt{a^2 - b^2}}{a}$.

44. Which of the following represents the graph of the equation $y = |x - 2|$?

(A)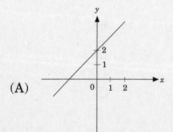

(B)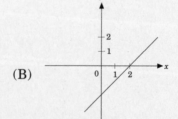

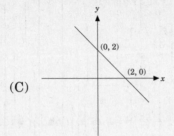

(C)

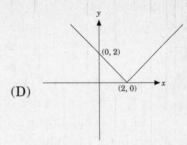

(D)

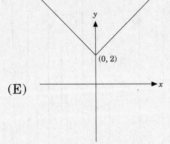

(E)

45. If $x \neq 0$, then $(3^{9x})(27^{2x}) =$

(A) 2^{5x}.

(D) 3^{18x}.

(B) 9^{3x}.

(E) 3^{9x}.

(C) 3^{15x}.

46. The perimeter of the regular hexagon is 30 cm. The area of the shaded region is

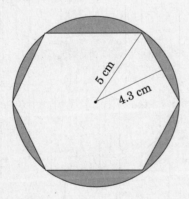

(A) 185 sq. cm.

(D) 14 sq. cm.

(B) 314 sq. cm.

(E) 250 sq. cm.

(C) 379 sq. cm.

47. If A can do a job in 8 days and B can do the same job in 12 days, how long would it take the two men working together?

(A) 3

(D) 5.8

(B) 4.8

(E) 6

(C) 10

48. If a sphere is inscribed into a cube of size 64 cubic inches, what is the volume of the sphere?

(A) $\dfrac{32}{3}\pi$

(D) $\dfrac{17}{3}\pi$

(B) $\dfrac{25}{3}\pi$

(E) $\dfrac{11}{3}\pi$

(C) $\dfrac{23}{3}\pi$

49. What are the coordinates of the point of intersection of the lines having equations

$$\sqrt{3}x + 2y = 1 \quad \text{and} \quad x - \sqrt{3}y = \sqrt{3}?$$

(A) $\left(\dfrac{2\sqrt{3}}{5}, \dfrac{3\sqrt{3}}{5}\right)$

(D) $\left(\dfrac{-2}{5}, \dfrac{3\sqrt{3}}{5}\right)$

(B) $\left(\dfrac{\sqrt{3}}{5}, -\dfrac{3}{5}\right)$

(E) $\left(\dfrac{3}{5}, \dfrac{2\sqrt{3}}{5}\right)$

(C) $\left(\dfrac{3\sqrt{3}}{5}, -\dfrac{2}{5}\right)$

50. In the figure, 0 is the center of the circle. If arc ABC has length 2π, what is the area of the circle?

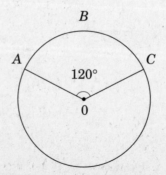

(A) 3π

(D) 12π

(B) 6π

(E) 15π

(C) 9π

TEST 3

ANSWER KEY

1. (D)	14. (B)	27. (A)	40. (E)
2. (C)	15. (D)	28. (C)	41. (A)
3. (D)	16. (B)	29. (B)	42. (C)
4. (A)	17. (B)	30. (A)	43. (B)
5. (B)	18. (A)	31. (C)	44. (D)
6. (D)	19. (D)	32. (D)	45. (C)
7. (A)	20. (C)	33. (A)	46. (D)
8. (C)	21. (A)	34. (B)	47. (B)
9. (E)	22. (B)	35. (E)	48. (A)
10. (C)	23. (C)	36. (B)	49. (C)
11. (A)	24. (B)	37. (D)	50. (C)
12. (E)	25. (D)	38. (A)	
13. (D)	26. (B)	39. (E)	

DETAILED EXPLANATIONS OF ANSWERS

1.   **(D)**

Substitute the values of x, a, b, c, and d into the expression.

$$z = \frac{(9 + 2(3.5)) \, (6 - 10)^2}{8^{\frac{1}{3}}}$$

$$= \frac{(9 + 7) \, (-4)^2}{8^{\frac{1}{3}}}$$

$$= \frac{(16) \, (16)}{8^{\frac{1}{3}}}$$

Calculator:

16 $\boxed{\times}$ 16 $\boxed{=}$ 256 $\boxed{\div}$ 8 $\boxed{y^x}$ $\boxed{(\,)}$ 1 $\boxed{\div}$ 3 $\boxed{(\,)}$ $\boxed{=}$ 128

2.   **(C)**

The total surface area is the sum of the surface areas of each side.

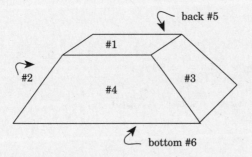

For side #1: $A = bh$

                        $= 6.7 \times 5.2$

Calculator:

6.7 $\boxed{\times}$ 5.2 $\boxed{=}$ 34.84

For sides #2 and #3, which are identical:

$$A = bh$$
$$= 5.2 \times 5.4$$

Calculator:

5.2 $\boxed{\times}$ 5.4 $\boxed{=}$ 28.08

For sides #4 and #5, which are identical, each area is:

$$A = \frac{1}{2}(b_1 + b_2)h \qquad\qquad b_1, b_2 \text{ are bases}$$

$$= \frac{1}{2} \times 5.0 \times (6.7 + 7.1)$$

Calculator:

.5 $\boxed{\times}$ 5.0 $\boxed{\times}$ $\boxed{()}$ 6.7 + 7.1 $\boxed{()}$ $\boxed{=}$ 34.50

For side #6: $\qquad A = bh$
$$= 7.1 \times 5.2$$

Calculator:

7.1 $\boxed{\times}$ 5.2 $\boxed{=}$ 36.92

Adding all sides together:

side #1 + side #2 + side #3 + side #4 + side #5 + side #6 = total area

Calculator:

34.84 $\boxed{+}$ 28.08 $\boxed{+}$ 28.08 $\boxed{+}$ 34.50 $\boxed{+}$ 34.50 $\boxed{+}$ 36.92 $\boxed{=}$ 196.92

3.   **(D)**

Cost of one chicken = $\dfrac{\$17.40}{12} = \$1.45$

Cost of one duck = $\$3.40 - \$1.45 = \$1.95$

4.   **(A)**

Substitute the values of x and y into the expression:

$$A = [(1.25)^2 + 3(1.25)(2.75) + 2(2.75)^2] \times [7(1.25)(2.75) - (2.75)^3]$$

Calculator:

1.25 $\boxed{x^2}$ = 1.5625

3 $\boxed{\times}$ 1.25 $\boxed{\times}$ 2.75 $\boxed{=}$ 10.3125

2.75 $\boxed{x^2}$ $\boxed{\times}$ 2 $\boxed{=}$ 15.13   and

7 $\boxed{\times}$ 1.25 $\boxed{(\,)}$ 2.75 $\boxed{=}$ 24.06

2.75 $\boxed{y^x}$ 3 $\boxed{=}$ 20.80

Calculator:

$A = 1.5625$ $\boxed{+}$ 10.3125 $\boxed{+}$ 15.125 $\boxed{=}$ 27 $\boxed{\times}$ $\boxed{(\,)}$ 24.0625 $\boxed{-}$ 20.7968 $\boxed{=}$ 88.17

5. **(B)**

$CD = BD - BC$

$CD = AB - BC$ $\qquad$ $(\because AB = BD)$

$CD = 4\dfrac{1}{2} - 2\dfrac{1}{4}$

$CD = 2\dfrac{1}{4}$

6. **(D)**

Distance between two points $= \sqrt{(x_1 - x_2)^2 + (y_1 - y_2)^2}$

$$= \sqrt{(0-7)^2 + (-2-0)^2}$$

$$= \sqrt{49 + 4}$$

$$= \sqrt{53}$$

7. **(A)**

Area of triangle $= \dfrac{1}{2}bh$. For a right triangle, the base and height are the legs which form the right angle. The lengths of the sides are:

$$DE = \sqrt{(-2.5 - 2.8)^2 + (2.8 - 1.2)^2}$$

Calculator:

2.5 $\boxed{+/-}$ $\boxed{-}$ 2.8 $\boxed{=}$ $\boxed{x^2}$ $\boxed{+}$ $\boxed{(\,)}$ 2.8 $\boxed{-}$ 1.2 $\boxed{(\,)}$ $\boxed{x^2}$ $\boxed{=}$ 30.7 $\boxed{\sqrt{}}$ $= 5.5$

$$\text{Area} = \frac{1}{2}bh$$

$$= \frac{1}{2}DE \times EF$$

$$= \frac{1}{2} \times 5.5 \times 4.4$$

$$= 12.1$$

$$EF = \sqrt{(2.8 - 2.0)^2 + (1.2 - (-3.1))^2}$$

Calculator:

$$2.8 \boxed{-} 2.0\boxed{=} 0.8\boxed{x^2} \boxed{+} \boxed{()} 1.2 \boxed{+} 3.1 \boxed{()} \boxed{x^2} \boxed{=} 1.913\boxed{\sqrt{}} = 4.4$$

8.   **(C)**

If $5 < a < 8$ and $6 < b < 9$, then ab will be bounded by (5×6) and (8×9).

9.   **(E)**

$$x° = y° \qquad\qquad (\because \text{ vertical angles})$$

$$x° + 70° = 180° \qquad\qquad (\because \text{ supplementary angles})$$

$$x° = 110°$$

$$\therefore x + y = 220° .$$

10.   **(C)**

$$\frac{a}{b} = 4 \qquad\qquad (\text{multiply both sides by } b)$$

$$a = 4b$$

$$a^2 - 16b^2 = (4b)^2 - 16b^2 \qquad (\text{substitute } a = 4b)$$

$$= 0$$

11.   **(A)**

Solve the equation simultaneously:

$$\begin{array}{ll} 5x - 3y = 16 \\ 2x + 7y = 12 \end{array} \Rightarrow \begin{array}{l} 10x - 6y = 32 \\ \underline{-10x - 35y = -60} \\ \quad\; -41y = -28 \end{array}$$

Calculator:

$$28 \boxed{+/-} \boxed{\div} 41 \boxed{+/-} \boxed{=} 0.683$$

$$\therefore y = 0.683$$

Solve for x:

$$5x - 3y = 16$$

$$x = \frac{16 + 3y}{5}$$

$$= \frac{16 + 3(0.683)}{5}$$

Calculator:

$$3 \boxed{\times} .683 \boxed{+} 16 \boxed{=} \boxed{\div} 5 \boxed{=} 3.610$$

$$(x, y) = (3.610, 0.683)$$

12. **(E)**

$$\frac{\frac{1}{b}}{3} = \frac{1}{4} \qquad \text{cross multiply}$$

$$\frac{b}{3} = 4 \qquad \text{cross multiply}$$

$$b = 12$$

13. **(D)**

$$\sqrt{8} + 3\sqrt{18} - 7\sqrt{2} = \sqrt{4} \times \sqrt{2} + 3\sqrt{9} \times \sqrt{2} - 7\sqrt{2}$$

$$= 2\sqrt{2} + 9\sqrt{2} - 7\sqrt{2}$$

$$= 4\sqrt{2}$$

14. **(E)**

Extend $\overline{RB}$ to meet line l at point E, then $\angle ARB$ and $\angle CER$ are alternate interior angles. Since r is parallel to l, it follows that the measure of $\angle ARB$ is equal to the measure of $\angle CER$. Thus, the measure of $\angle CER = 55°$.

Since $\angle RBC$ is an exterior angle of triangle BEC, and the measure of an exterior angle of a triangle is equal to the sum of the measures of the two non-adjacent interior angles of the triangles, it follows that the measure of $\angle RBC$ is equal to the sum of the measures of $\angle BEC$ and $\angle BCE$. Thus,

$$\angle RBC = 55° + 25° = 80°$$

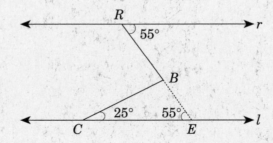

15.   **(D)**

Substitute $x = 2$ and $y = 1$ into the pair of equations to obtain:

$$2a + b = 8$$

$$a + 2b = 10$$

Multiply the second equation by –2 and add it to the first equation to solve for b.

$$\begin{array}{r} 2a + b = 8 \\ -2a - 4b = -20 \\ \hline -3b = -12 \\ b = 4 \end{array}$$

Substituting 4 back into equation 1 yields:

$$2a + 4 = 8$$

$$2a = 4$$

$$a = 2$$

16.   **(B)**

The distance formula is:

$$d = \sqrt{(x_2 - x_1)^2 + (y_2 - y_1)^2}$$

$$= \sqrt{(3 - (-4))^2 + (4 - (-1))^2}$$

$$= \sqrt{(3 + 4)^2 + (4 + 1)^2}$$

Calculator:

$3 \boxed{+} 4 \boxed{=} 7 \boxed{x^2} \boxed{=} 49 \boxed{+} \boxed{(\,)} 4 \boxed{+} 1 \boxed{(\,)} \boxed{x^2} \boxed{=} 74 \boxed{\sqrt{}} = 8.60$

17. **(B)**

$\angle ACB = \angle ABC = 45°$ because $AB = AC$ (isosceles triangle)

$\angle CAB = 180° - \angle ABC - \angle ACB$

$= 180° - 90° = 90°$

Therefore, $\triangle ABC$ is a right triangle.

Use Pythagoras' theorem:

$$BC = \sqrt{AB^2 + AC^2}$$

$$= \sqrt{3^2 + 3^2}$$

$$= 3\sqrt{2}$$

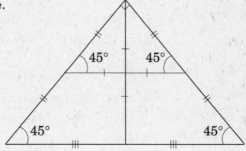

18. **(A)**

Let $f^{-1}(b) = a$ if and only if $f(a) = b$. Solve for a in terms of b to get f^{-1}.

$$f(x) = 4.3x - 5.4$$

$$f(a) = 4.3a - 5.4$$

$$b = 4.3a - 5.4$$

$$f^{-1}(a) = \frac{b + 5.4}{4.3}$$

$$f^{-1}(x) = \frac{x + 5.4}{4.3}$$

$$f^{-1}(9.2) = \frac{9.2 + 5.4}{4.3}$$

Calculator:

9.2 $\boxed{+}$ 5.4 $\boxed{=}$ $\boxed{\div}$ 4.3 $\boxed{=}$ 3.39 (or 3.40)

19. **(D)**

Evaluate the function

$$f(3) = 3^5 - 3 \times 3^4 + 4 \times 3^2 - 6 \times 3 + 7$$

Calculator:

3 $\boxed{y^x}$ 5 $\boxed{-}$ 3 $\boxed{\times}$ 3 $\boxed{y^x}$ 4 $\boxed{+}$ 4 $\boxed{\times}$ 3 $\boxed{x^2}$ $\boxed{-}$ 6 $\boxed{\times}$ 3 $\boxed{+}$ 7 $\boxed{=}$ 25

20.   **(C)**

$AB = AC = 4$ because $\triangle ABC$ is an isosceles triangle.

$$\text{Area of } \triangle ABC = \frac{1}{2} \, (4) \, (4)$$

$$= 8$$

$$\text{Area of } \triangle ADB = \frac{1}{2} \, (4) \, (7)$$

$$= 14$$

$$\text{Area of } \triangle DCB = \text{area of } \triangle ADB - \text{area of } \triangle ABC$$

$$= 14 - 8$$

$$= 6$$

21.   **(A)**

$$g(2) = \frac{1}{3(2)} = \frac{1}{6}$$

$$f(g(2)) = f\left(\frac{1}{6}\right) = \frac{2\left(\frac{1}{6}\right) - 1}{\frac{1}{6}} = -4$$

22.   **(B)**

Solve for x.

$$\sqrt[6]{x^2} = \sqrt[3]{b}$$

$$x^2 = (\sqrt[3]{b})^6$$

$$x = \sqrt{(\sqrt[3]{b})^6}$$

$$= \sqrt{(\sqrt[3]{25})^6} = \sqrt{(25)^{\frac{6}{3}}} = \sqrt{(25)^2} = 25$$

Calculator:

25 $\boxed{y^x}$ $\boxed{(\,)}$ 1 $\boxed{\div}$ 3 $\boxed{(\,)}$ $\boxed{=}$ $\boxed{y^x}$ 6 $\boxed{=}$ $\boxed{\sqrt{}}$ $= 25$

23.   **(C)**

The lengths of corresponding sides are proportional. Thus:

$$\frac{16.3}{4.0} = \frac{14.4}{k}$$

$$k = \frac{4\,(14.4)}{16.3}$$

Calculator:

4 $\boxed{\times}$ 14.41 $\boxed{\div}$ 16.3 $\boxed{=}$ 3.53

24.   **(B)**

$$8a + 12b = c$$

$$4\,(2a + 3b) = c$$

Only 4 can be factored out.

25.   **(D)**

Write in terms of logarithms.

$$(x - 1)\log 9.04 = x\log 4.37$$

$$\frac{x - 1}{x} = \frac{\log 4.37}{\log 9.04}$$

Calculator:

4.37 $\boxed{\log}$ $\boxed{\div}$ 9.04 $\boxed{\log}$ $\boxed{=}$ 0.6698

$$\frac{x - 1}{x} = 0.6698$$

$$x = \frac{1}{1 - 0.6698}$$

Calculator:

1 $\boxed{-}$ 0.6698 $\boxed{=}$ $\boxed{1/x}$ = 3.0285

26.   **(B)**

$$\cos A = \frac{AB}{AC} = \frac{12}{13}$$

$$BC = \sqrt{(AC)^2 - (AB)^2}$$

$$= \sqrt{13^2 - 12^2}$$

$$= \sqrt{25} = 5$$

27.   **(A)**

(D) and (E) are not functions. (B) and (C) are functions but not one-to-one, because each y-value corresponds to two x-values instead of one. However, (A) is.

28.   **(C)**

Volume of the cube $= s^3$

Volume of the sphere $= \dfrac{4}{3}\pi r^3$

Since the sphere is inscribed in the cube, the diameter of the sphere is equal to the length of a side, therefore the radius is half the diameter.

$$\text{Ratio:} \; = \frac{\dfrac{4}{3}\pi \left(\dfrac{s}{2}\right)^3}{s^3}$$

$$= \frac{\dfrac{4}{3}\pi \left(\dfrac{20}{2}\right)^3}{20^3}$$

Calculator:

$$4 \;\boxed{\div}\; 3 \;\boxed{\times}\; \pi \;\boxed{\times}\; 10 \;\boxed{y^x}\; 3 \;\boxed{=}\; 4189 \;\boxed{\div}\; \boxed{(} \;20\; \boxed{y^x}\; 3 \;\boxed{)}\; \boxed{=}\; 0.524$$

29.   **(B)**

The area of the circle is πr^2. To find the length of the radius, determine the distance between D and E.

$$2 = DE = \sqrt{(6-4)^2 + (7-5)^2}$$

Calculator:

$$6 \;\boxed{-}\; 4 \;\boxed{=}\; \boxed{x^2}\; \boxed{+}\; \boxed{(}\; 7 \;\boxed{-}\; 5 \;\boxed{)}\; \boxed{x^2}\; \boxed{=}\; \boxed{\sqrt{}}\; \boxed{=}\; 2.83$$

Area $= \pi\,(2.83)^2$

Calculator:

$$2.83 \; \boxed{x^2} \; \boxed{\times} \; \pi \; \boxed{=} \; 25.2$$

30. **(A)**

The denominators of the fractions cannot be zero. Hence, the values which b cannot have are:

$$b^3 - 8 = 0$$

$$b = \sqrt[3]{8}$$

Calculator:

$$8 \; \boxed{y^x} \; \boxed{(\,)} \; 1 \; \boxed{\div} \; 3 \; \boxed{(\,)} \; \boxed{=} \; 2.00$$

$$b^5 - 5 = 0$$

$$b = \sqrt[5]{5}$$

Calculator:

$$5 \; \boxed{y^x} \; \boxed{(\,)} \; 1 \; \boxed{\div} \; 5 \; \boxed{(\,)} \; \boxed{=} \; 1.38$$

$$b^2 - 7 = 0$$

$$b = \sqrt{7}$$

Calculator:

$$7 \; \boxed{\sqrt{}} \; = \; \pm 2.65$$

Thus, 2.00, 1.38, and ± 2.65 cannot be roots of the equation.

31. **(C)**

$$G : (2,\, 4) = \left(\frac{2^3}{5}, \; \frac{2 \times 4 - 5 \times 2^2}{4} \right)$$

Calculator (for first term):

$$2 \; \boxed{y^x} \; 3 \; \boxed{\div} \; 5 \; \boxed{=} \; 1.6$$

Calculator (for second term):

$$2 \; \boxed{\times} \; 4 \; \boxed{-} \; 5 \; \boxed{\times} \; 2 \; \boxed{x^2} \; \boxed{=} \; -12 \; \boxed{\div} \; 4 \; \boxed{=} \; -3$$

$$G : (2,\, 4) = (1.6,\, -3)$$

32.   **(D)**

If $\cos\beta = 0.5$, then $\beta = \cos^{-1}(0.5)$

Calculator:

$0.5 \boxed{\times} \cos^{-1} = 60°$

and $\alpha + \beta = 360°$

$$\alpha = 360° - \beta = 360° - 60° = 300°$$

$$\tan\alpha = \tan 300°$$

Calculator:

$300° \boxed{\tan} = -1.732$

33.   **(A)**

Let $y = f(x) = 3x + 2$.

Then, $x = \dfrac{y-2}{3}$

Therefore, $g(x) = \dfrac{x-2}{3}$.

34.   **(B)**

$\Delta DEG \cong \Delta ABG, \quad \Delta GEF \cong \Delta GBC, \quad \text{and} \quad \Delta GDF \cong \Delta GAC$

Therefore,

$$\frac{AB}{AC} = \frac{DE}{DF} = \frac{DE}{DE+EF} = \frac{a}{a+b}$$

35.   **(E)**

This is a quadratic equation:

$$ax^2 + bx + c = 0, \text{ with } a = 2.4,\ b = -7.3,\ c = 5.3$$

Using the quadratic formula:

$$x = \frac{-b \pm \sqrt{b^2 - 4ac}}{2a}$$

To solve for x:

$$x = \frac{-(-7.3) \pm \sqrt{(-7.3)^2 - 4\,(2.4)\,(5.3)}}{2\,(2.4)}$$

Evaluate the expression under the $\sqrt{\ }$.

Calculator:

7.3 $\boxed{+/-}$ $\boxed{x^2}$ $\boxed{-}$ 4 $\boxed{\times}$ 2.4 $\boxed{\times}$ 5.3 $\boxed{=}$ 2.41 $\boxed{\sqrt{}}$ = 1.55

Thus, $\qquad x = \dfrac{7.3 + 1.55}{2\,(2.4)}$

Calculator:

7.3 $\boxed{+}$ 1.55 $\boxed{=}$ 8.85 $\boxed{\div}$ 2 $\boxed{\div}$ 2.4 $\boxed{=}$ 1.84

and $\qquad x = \dfrac{7.3 - 1.55}{2\,(2.4)}$

Calculator:

7.3 $\boxed{-}$ 1.55 $\boxed{=}$ 5.75 $\boxed{\div}$ 2 $\boxed{\div}$ 2.4 $\boxed{=}$ 1.20

36.　　**(B)**

The diameter of the inscribed circle is x. Therefore, the circumference of the inscribed circle $= x\pi$.

The diameter of circumscribed circle is $\sqrt{x^2 + x^2} = x\sqrt{2}$. Therefore, its circumference is $x\pi\sqrt{2}$.

The ratio: $\dfrac{\text{circumference of circumscribed circle}}{\text{circumference of inscribed circle}}$

$$= \frac{x\pi\sqrt{2}}{x\pi} = \sqrt{2}$$

37.　　**(D)**

$$\frac{y-4}{x-1} = \frac{4-2}{1-3}$$

$$\frac{y-4}{x-1} = -1$$

$$y - 4 = -x + 1$$

$$y = -x + 5$$

Therefore, the y-intercept is 5.

38.   **(A)**

$$\frac{1}{2x} = \frac{1}{\frac{1}{y}}$$

$$\frac{1}{2x} = y$$

For $x = 1$, $y = \dfrac{1}{2}$

for $x = 5$, $y = \dfrac{1}{10}$.

Therefore, $0.1 < y < 0.5$

39.   **(E)**

$$\text{weight} = \text{density} \times \text{volume}$$

Thus, ratio of weight is the same as the ratio of volume.

$$\text{ratio of volume} = (\text{ratio of radii})^3$$

$$= \left(\frac{2}{3}\right)^3$$

$$= \frac{8}{27}$$

40.   **(E)**

I.   From Pythagoras's theorem, $c = \sqrt{a^2 + b^2}$

II. $\cos\theta = \dfrac{b}{c}$

$$c = \frac{b}{\cos\theta}$$

III. $\sin\phi = \dfrac{b}{c}$

$$c = \frac{b}{\sin\phi}$$

Therefore, I, II, and III are true.

41.　**(A)**

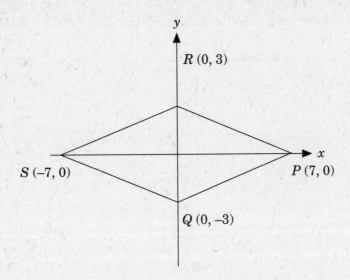

Area of $PQRS = 4 \times \dfrac{1}{2} \times 3 \times 7 = 42$

42.　**(C)**

In order for two dice to sum up to 10, either the first die is a four and the second is a six, they are both five's, or the first one is a six and the second is a four. So there are only three possibilities out of 36 possible outcomes which is

$$\frac{3}{36} = \frac{1}{12} \; .$$

43.　**(B)**

$\sin^2 \theta + \cos^2 \theta = 1$ 　　　　　Trigonometric identity

$$\sin \theta = \sqrt{1 - \cos^2 \theta}$$

$$= \sqrt{1 - \left(\frac{a}{b}\right)^2}$$

$$= \frac{\sqrt{b^2 - a^2}}{b}$$

44. **(D)**

By setting $x - 2$ equal to zero we find our x and y-coordinates, $(2, 0)$ and $(0, 2)$. By substituting in other points we will have the graph shown in (D).

45. **(C)**

$$(3^{9x})(27^{2x}) = (3^{9x})(3^3)^{2x}$$

$$= (3^{9x})(3^{6x})$$

$$= 3^{9x+6x}$$

$$= 3^{15x}$$

46. **(D)**

Shaded area = area of the circle − area of the hexagon

Area of the circle = πr^2

Area of hexagon = $6 \times$ area of each triangle

$$= 6 \times \frac{1}{2}bh$$

$$= 6 \times \frac{1}{2} \times 5 \times 4.3$$

Shaded area = $\pi \times 5^2 - 6 \times 0.5 \times 5 \times 4.3$

Calculator:

$\pi \boxed{\times} 5 \boxed{x^2} \boxed{=} 78.54 \boxed{-} 6 \boxed{\times} .5 \boxed{\times} 5 \boxed{\times} 4.3 \boxed{=} 14$

47. **(B)**

Let x = the number of days it would take the two men working together.

Then $\dfrac{x}{8}$ = the part of the job done by A and $\dfrac{x}{12}$ = the part of the job done by B. The relationship used in setting up the equation is:

Part of job done by A + part of job done by B = 1 job

$$\frac{x}{8} + \frac{x}{12} = 1.$$

$$3x + 2x = 24$$

$$5x = 24$$

$$x = 4.8 \ .$$

48.   **(A)**

Diameter of the sphere $= \sqrt[3]{64} = 4$

Volume of the sphere $= \dfrac{4}{3}\pi r^3$

$$= \dfrac{4}{3}\pi \left(\dfrac{4}{2}\right)^3$$

$$= \dfrac{32\pi}{3}$$

49.   **(C)**

$$\begin{cases} \sqrt{3}x + 2y = 1 & \quad (1) \\ x - \sqrt{3}y = \sqrt{3} & \quad (2) \end{cases}$$

$(1) - (2) \times \sqrt{3}$

$$\begin{array}{r} \sqrt{3}x + 2y = 1 \\ -\left(\sqrt{3}x - 3y = 3\right) \\ \hline 5y = -2 \\ y = -\dfrac{2}{5} \end{array}$$

Only (C) has $\dfrac{-2}{5}$ as the y-coordinate.

50.   **(C)**

$$\dfrac{2\pi}{120°} = \dfrac{2\pi r}{360°}$$

$$r = 3$$

Area $= \pi r^2 = 9\pi$

THE SAT SUBJECT TEST IN

Math
Level 1

PRACTICE TEST 4

SAT Mathematics
Level 1

Practice Test 4

Time: 1 Hour
50 Questions

DIRECTIONS: Choose the best answer for each question and mark the letter of your selection on the corresponding answer sheet.

NOTES:

(1) Some questions require the use of a calculator. You must decide when the use of your calculator will be helpful.

(2) Make sure your calculator is in degree mode.

(3) All figures are drawn to scale and lie in a plane unless otherwise stated.

(4) The domain of any function f is the set of all real numbers x for which $f(x)$ is a real number, unless other information is provided.

REFERENCE INFORMATION: The following information may be helpful in answering some of the questions.

Volume of a right circular cone with radius r and height h	$V = \dfrac{1}{3}\pi r^2 h$
Lateral area of a right circular cone with circumference c and slant height l	$S = \dfrac{1}{2}cl$
Volume of a sphere with radius r	$V = \dfrac{4}{3}\pi r^3$
Surface area of a sphere with radius r	$S = 4\pi r^2$
Volume of a pyramid with base area B and height h	$V = \dfrac{1}{3}Bh$

---

1.   In triangle *ABC,* angle *A* is a right angle, and the length of *BC* is 7. What are the lengths of sides *AB* and *AC*?

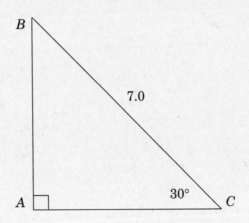

(A)   4.9, 4.9   (D)   3.5, 6.1

(B)   2.0, 6.1   (E)   4.9, 6.1

(C)   3.5, 4.9

2.   Let $n(A)$ denote the number of elements in set *A*. If $n(A) = 10$, $n(B) = 12$, and $n(A \cap B) = 3$, how many elements does $A \cup B$ contain?

(A)   10   (D)   19

(B)   12   (E)   22

(C)   15

3.   If $A \subset C$ and $B \subset C$, which of the following statements are true?

(A)   The set $A \cup B$ is also a subset of *C*.

(B)   The complement of *A* is also a subset of *C*.

(C)   The complement of *B* is also a subset of *C*.

(D)   The union of $\overline{A}$ and $\overline{B}$ contains *C*.

(E)   *C* is the universal set.

4. Circle O has an inscribed triangle AOB. Find the measure of angle x.

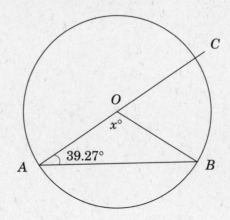

(A) 101.46°

(D) 62.19°

(B) 39.27°

(E) 140.73°

(C) 60.73°

5. Evaluate

$$\sqrt[7]{(x+3.65)^5 + x^{\frac{1}{3}}}$$

with $x = 3.14$.

(A) 2.52×10^0

(D) 2.55×10^8

(B) 1.48×10^0

(E) 1.32×10^6

(C) 3.93×10^0

6. Given the expression:

$$(y^2 + 4) = \sqrt[3]{(x^3 + 2)^5} + 7$$

and $y = 9$, find x.

(A) 3.52

(D) 2.31

(B) 12.38

(E) 3.79

(C) 2.43

7. Find the value of x.

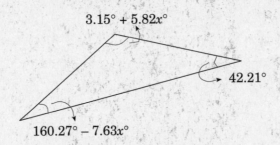

$$3.15° + 5.82x°$$

$$42.21°$$

$$160.27° - 7.63x°$$

(A) 19.08°

(B) 14.16°

(C) 36.46°

(D) 16.14°

(E) 53.24°

8. If $x = 1$, and $y = -2$, then $3x^2y - 2xy^2 + 5xy =$

(A) 6.

(B) 9.

(C) -24.

(D) -12.

(E) -15.

9. If $g(x) = x^2 + 5x - 3$, then $g(-7) =$

(A) -7.

(B) -5.

(C) 7.

(D) 9.

(E) 11.

10. Triangle ABC is similar to triangle ADE. If the area of triangle ABC is 324, the area of triangle ADE is 441, and $AC = 36$, what is the length of $\overline{CE}$?

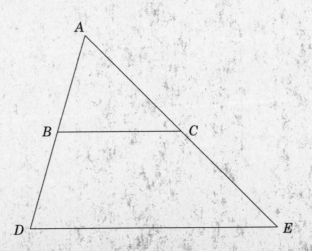

(A) 22

(D) 42

(B) 6

(E) 14

(C) 49

11. In the triangle below, the measure of angle x is:

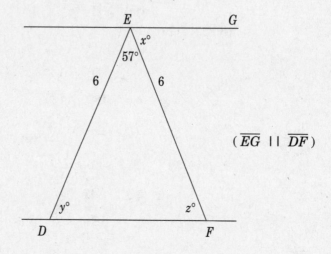

$(\overline{EG} \; || \; \overline{DF})$

(A) 33.0°

(D) 28.5°

(B) 61.5°

(E) 57.0°

(C) 59.0°

12. If $\vec{A} = 2 + 3i$ and $\vec{B} = -1 + 2i$, then $\vec{A} + \vec{B} =$

(A) $2 + 5i$

(D) $3 + 2i$

(B) $1 + 5i$

(E) $3 + 5i$

(C) $3 + i$

13. If $AC \perp CB$, then what is the abscissa of point B?

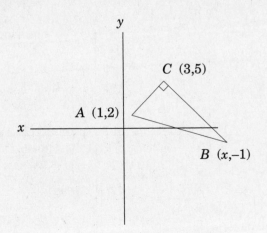

(A) −1   (D) 12

(B) 0   (E) 6

(C) 5

14. A bag contains four white balls, six black balls, three red balls, and eight green balls. If one ball is drawn from the bag, find the probability that it will be either white or green.

(A) $\dfrac{1}{3}$ (D) $\dfrac{4}{13}$

(B) $\dfrac{2}{3}$ (E) $\dfrac{8}{21}$

(C) $\dfrac{4}{7}$

15. A box contains 30 yellow balls, 40 green balls, and 15 red balls. What is the probability of choosing a red ball first followed by a yellow ball with no replacement?

(A) 0.3571   (D) 0.0620

(B) 0.1765   (E) 0.0630

(C) 0.3529

16. Which of the following equations corresponds to the graph below?

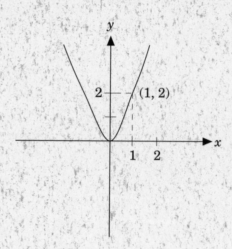

(A) $y = x^2$

(B) $y = 2x^2$

(C) $y = 2x^2 + 1$

(D) $y = 2(x^2 + 1)$

(E) $y = 2(x^2 - 1)$

17. $f(x) = x^2 + 2x - 5$ has the domain $\{0, 1, 2, 3\}$. What value is not in the range of $f(x)$?

(A) 1

(B) –5

(C) 3

(D) –3

(E) 10

18. In the figure below, if $\overline{AD}$ crosses $\overline{BC}$ at the center of the circle at E, then $\angle CBD =$

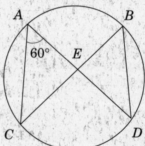

(A) 30°.

(B) 60°,

(C) 90°.

(D) 120°.

(E) 135°.

19. If a binary operation $\oplus$ is defined for all real numbers a and b by the equation $a \oplus b = 2ab + b$, then $3 \oplus (-2) =$

(A) 1.

(D) –14.

(B) 3.

(E) –6.

(C) 6.

20. The area of the shape below is 150 cm². Find the value of a if $x = 4.5$.

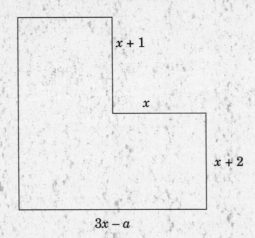

$x + 1$

x

$x + 2$

$3x - a$

(A) 13.38

(D) –13.38

(B) 1.00

(E) 1.06

(C) –1.06

21. What value of m is a root of the equation shown below?

$$3m = 2m^2 - 1$$

(A) –1.78

(D) 0.00

(B) 0.28

(E) –0.28

(C) 1.00

22. If a line contains the points $(1, 2)$ and $(3, 4)$, then its x-intercept is

(A) –1.

(D) 2.

(B) 0.

(E) 3.

(C) 1.

23. In the figure below, if $CD \parallel AB$ and $\dfrac{CD}{AB} = \dfrac{1}{2}$, then what is the ratio of the area of $\triangle CED$ to the area of $\triangle AEB$?

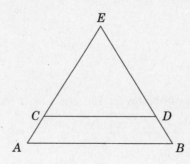

(A) $\dfrac{1}{8}$ (D) 2

(B) $\dfrac{1}{4}$ (E) 4

(C) $\dfrac{1}{2}$

24. What is the volume of the shaded region?

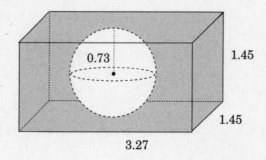

(A) 1.21 (D) 0.18

(B) 5.25 (E) 6.50

(C) 11.21

25. If $f(x) = 2x + 3$ and $g(x) = \dfrac{1}{3x}$, then $f(g(5)) =$

(A) $\dfrac{1}{3}$. (D) $3\dfrac{2}{15}$.

(B) $\dfrac{1}{15}$. (E) $3\dfrac{2}{3}$.

(C) $3\dfrac{1}{3}$.

26. If $0° \le \theta \le 90°$, the value of $2\cos^2\theta + 2\sin^2\theta$ is

    (A) $\cos^2\theta$.   (D) $2\sin\theta$.

    (B) $\sin^2\theta$.   (E) 2.

    (C) $2\cos\theta$.

27. Given the group of numbers:

    $$72, 75, 83, 83, 86, 92, 97$$

    Which of the following statements are true?

    I.   The mean is 86.

    II. The median is 84.

    III. The mode is 83.

    (A) I only.   (D) I and II only.

    (B) II only.   (E) All statements are true.

    (C) III only.

28. Tanβ is:

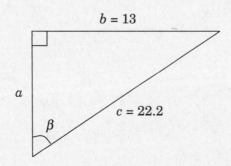

    (A) 0.5855   (D) 0.8107

    (B) −0.7222   (E) 0.7222

    (C) −0.5855

29. If $g(x) = \sqrt{x}$ and $f(x) = \dfrac{x^3 - 5x + 9}{25x^4}$, what is $g(f(4))$?

    (A) 0.033   (D) 0.910

    (B) 0.008   (E) 0.091

    (C) 0.207

30. If $x \neq 0$, then $(2^{4x})(8^{2x}) =$

    (A) 16^{3x}.

    (D) 2^{16x}.

    (B) 2^{10x}.

    (E) 16^{2x}.

    (C) 4^{4x}.

31. If $y = 2(x - 3)^2$ and $x = -1$, then $y =$

    (A) 4.

    (D) 32.

    (B) 8.

    (E) 48.

    (C) 16.

32. If $ab - 3 = 7$ and $b - 2 = 3$, then $a =$

    (A) −1.

    (D) 4.

    (B) 2.

    (E) 5.

    (C) 3.

33. Which of the following represents the graph of $y = 2x + 1$?

(A)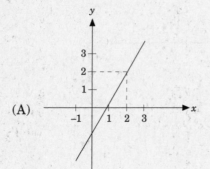

(B)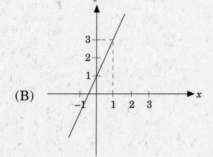

(C)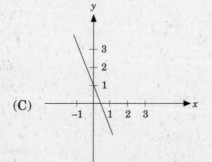

(D)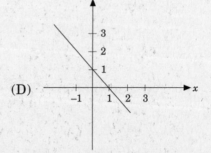

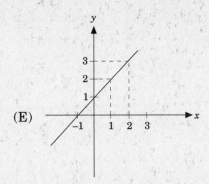

(E)

34. If the cost of a dozen pencils and a dozen pens together is $16.20, and if the cost of a pencil is $0.15, what is the cost of a pen?

(A) $1.20

(D) $1.55

(B) $1.35

(E) $1.60

(C) $1.40

35. What is the surface area of a sphere with diameter 10?

(A) 60π

(D) 120π

(B) 80π

(E) 140π

(C) 100π

36. Find the coordinates of the intersection of the following two lines: $x + 2y = 5$ and $2x + 3y = 2$.

(A) $(-12, 6)$

(D) $(10, 10)$

(B) $(-11, 8)$

(E) $(11, 12)$

(C) $(-10, 9)$

37. If $\alpha = 63.7°$, what is the length of a?

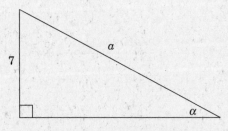

(A) 15.80

(D) 0.13

(B) 7.81

(E) 5.21

(C) 8.70

38. Find the constant A so that the lines $3x - 4y = 12$ and $Ax + 6y = -9$ are parallel.

(A) $-\dfrac{9}{2}$ (D) $\dfrac{7}{2}$

(B) $-\dfrac{7}{2}$ (E) $\dfrac{9}{2}$

(C) $\dfrac{5}{2}$

39. Find the solution set of the inequality $2x + 5 > 11$.

(A) $x < 6$ (D) $x < -3$

(B) $x > 3$ (E) $x > 6$

(C) $x = 3$

40. If $a = 3 + 2i$ and $b = 1 + 4i$ and $i = \sqrt{-1}$, then $ab =$

(A) $4 + 6i$.   (D) $-6 + 13i$.

(B) $1 + 2i$.   (E) $6 + 14i$.

(C) $-5 + 14i$.

41. In the figure, C is the midpoint of segment AD, $BC = CD$, and $\angle BCD = 70°$, therefore $\theta =$

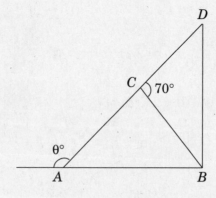

(A) $110°$.   (D) $145°$.

(B) $125°$.   (E) $160°$.

(C) $130°$.

42. Solution A is 30% acid and solution B is 65% acid. If you mix both together, then how many liters of solution B are needed to make 10 liters of a 46% acid solution?

(A) 4.57

(D) 2.92

(B) 7.08

(E) 15.38

(C) 5.43

43. If $a^2b^3 = 3^7$ and $a = 9$, then $b =$

(A) 1

(D) 3

(B) 2

(E) $3\sqrt{3}$

(C) $\sqrt{3}$

44. When rolling a six-sided die, what is the probability of getting either a four or five?

(A) 0.5000

(D) 0.1670

(B) 0.3333

(E) 3.0000

(C) 0.2500

45. If $f(x) = 3x + 4$ for all x, then the slope of the line $y = f(x + 3)$ is

(A) 3.

(D) 6.

(B) 4.

(E) 9.

(C) 5.

46. Find the equation of a line which passes through the point $(-1, 2)$ and intersects the y-axis at $y = 3$.

(A) $y = 2x + 3$

(D) $y = 3x$

(B) $y = x + 3$

(E) $y = 3x - 3$

(C) $y = x - 3$

47. If $x + yi = (3 + 2i)(1 + 3i)$ and $i = \sqrt{-1}$, then $x =$

(A) -3.

(D) 6.

(B) -1.

(E) 9.

(C) 3.

48. Find all the roots of the equation $(x + 1)(x^2 + 4x - 5) = 0$.

(A) $\{-1, 4, -5\}$

(D) $\{1, 4, 5\}$

(B) $\{1, 2, 3\}$

(E) $\{-1, 2, 3\}$

(C) $\{-5, -1, 1\}$

49. Triangle RST is shown in the figure below. U is the midpoint of RS. The coordinates of U are:

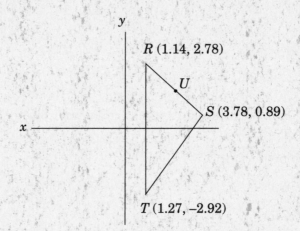

(A) $(1.84, 2.46)$.

(D) $(2.60, 2.46)$.

(B) $(1.20, -0.07)$.

(E) $(2.56, -0.60)$.

(C) $(2.46, 1.84)$.

50. If $\dfrac{3}{x+2} = \dfrac{5}{x+7}$, then $x =$

(A) $\dfrac{7}{2}$.

(D) $\dfrac{13}{2}$.

(B) $\dfrac{9}{2}$.

(E) $\dfrac{15}{2}$.

(C) $\dfrac{11}{2}$.

TEST 4

ANSWER KEY

1. (D)	14. (C)	27. (C)	40. (C)
2. (D)	15. (E)	28. (E)	41. (D)
3. (A)	16. (B)	29. (E)	42. (A)
4. (A)	17. (A)	30. (B)	43. (D)
5. (C)	18. (B)	31. (D)	44. (B)
6. (D)	19. (D)	32. (B)	45. (A)
7. (B)	20. (C)	33. (B)	46. (B)
8. (C)	21. (E)	34. (A)	47. (A)
9. (E)	22. (A)	35. (C)	48. (C)
10. (B)	23. (B)	36. (B)	49. (C)
11. (B)	24. (B)	37. (B)	50. (C)
12. (B)	25. (D)	38. (A)	
13. (D)	26. (E)	39. (B)	

DETAILED EXPLANATIONS
OF ANSWERS

1. **(D)**

This is a 30°, 60°, and 90° triangle. The hypotenuse (BC) is twice the length of the shorter leg (AB), and the length of the longer leg (AC) is the length of the shorter leg multiplied by $\sqrt{3}$.

$$2AB = BC$$

$$AB = \frac{BC}{2}$$

$$AB = \frac{7.0}{2} = 3.5$$

and

$$AC = \sqrt{3} \times AB$$

$$= \sqrt{3} \times 3.5$$

Calculator:

3 $\boxed{\sqrt{}}$ $\boxed{\times}$ 3.5 $\boxed{=}$ 6.1

2. **(D)**

$$n(A \cup B) = n(A) + n(B) - n(A \cap B)$$

$$= 10 + 12 - 3$$

$$= 19$$

3. **(A)**

The set $A \cup B$ contains all elements which belong to either set A or set B. Since all elements which belong to set A or B also belong to C, the set $A \cup B$ is a subset of C.

4. **(A)**

Triangle AOB has sides AO and OB which are both radii of circle O. Therefore, $\overline{AO} = \overline{OB}$ and then $\angle OAB = \angle OBA$. The sum of the angles of the triangle is equal to 180°.

$$\angle x° + \angle OAB° + \angle OBA° = 180°$$
$$\angle x° = 180° - \angle OAB° - \angle OBA°$$
$$= 180° - 39.27° - 39.27°$$
$$= 101.46°$$

5.　　**(C)**

Substitute the value for x in the expression:

$$\sqrt[7]{(3.14+3.65)^5 +(3.14)^{\frac{1}{3}}}$$

Calculator:

3.14 ⊞ 3.65 ⊟ 6.79 $\boxed{y^x}$ 5 = 14432.74 ⊞ 3.14 $\boxed{y^x}$ ⬚ 1 ⊟ 3 ⬚ ⊟ 14434.20 $\boxed{y^x}$ ⬚ 1 ⊟ 7 ⬚ ⊟ 3.93

6.　　**(D)**

Solve the equation for x

$$\sqrt[3]{(x^3 +2)^5 +7} = y^2 +4$$

$$(x^3 +2)^5 +7 = (y^2 +4)^3$$

$$(x^3 +2)^5 = (y^2 +4)^3 -7$$

$$x^3 +2 = \sqrt[5]{(y^2 +4)^3 -7}$$

$$x = \sqrt[3]{\sqrt[5]{(y^2 +4)^3 -7} -2}$$

Substitute the value for y.

$$x = \sqrt[3]{\sqrt[5]{(9^2 +4)^3 -7} -2}$$

Calculator:

9 $\boxed{x^2}$ ⊞ 4 ⊟ 85 $\boxed{y^x}$ 3 ⊟ 7 ⊟ $\boxed{y^x}$ ⬚ 1 ⊟ 5 ⬚ ⊟ 14.38 ⊟ 2 ⊟ 12.38 $\boxed{y^x}$ ⬚ 1 ⊟ 3 ⬚ ⊟ 2.31

7. **(B)**

The sum of all interior angles of a triangle is 180°. Thus:

$$3.15° + 5.82x° + 42.21° + 160.27° - 7.63x = 180°$$

Rearranging the equation:

$$5.82x° - 7.63x = 180° - 3.15° - 42.21° - 160.27°$$

$$x = \frac{180° - 3.15° - 42.21° - 160.27°}{(5.82 - 7.63)°}$$

Calculator:

180 $\boxed{-}$ 3.15 $\boxed{-}$ 42.21 $\boxed{-}$ 160.27 $\boxed{=}$ −25.63 $\boxed{\div}$ $\boxed{(\ )}$ 5.82 $\boxed{-}$ 7.63 $\boxed{(\ )}$ $\boxed{=}$ 14.16°

8. **(C)**

$$3x^2y - 2xy^2 + 5xy = xy(3x - 2y + 5)$$

$$= (1)(-2)(3 + 4 + 5)$$

$$= (-2)(12)$$

$$= -24$$

9. **(E)**

$$g(-7) = (-7)^2 + 5(-7) - 3$$

$$= 49 - 35 - 3$$

$$= 11$$

10. **(B)**

The ratio of the area of two similar polygons is equal to the square of the ratio of the lengths of any two corresponding sides. Thus:

$$\frac{\text{Area } \triangle ABC}{\text{Area } \triangle ADE} = \left(\frac{AC}{AE}\right)^2$$

$$(AE)^2 = \frac{(AC)^2 (\text{Area } \triangle ADE)}{\text{Area } \triangle ABC}$$

$$AE = \sqrt{\frac{(AC)^2 \ (\text{Area } \triangle ADE)}{\text{Area } \triangle ABC}}$$

$$= \sqrt{36^2 \left(\frac{441}{324}\right)}$$

Calculator:

$$441 \ \boxed{\div} \ 324 \ \boxed{\times} \ 36 \ \boxed{x^2} \ \boxed{=} \ 1764 \ \boxed{\sqrt{\ }} = 42$$

Thus, $AE = 42$. Since $AC + CE = AE$, then

$$CE = AE - AC$$

$$= 42 - 36$$

$$= 6$$

11.   **(B)**

Triangle DEF has two equal sides and therefore $\angle y = \angle z$. The sum of the angles of a triangle is 180°.

$$57° + \angle y + \angle z = 180°$$

$$\angle z + \angle z = 180° - 57°$$

$$\angle z = \frac{180° - 57°}{2}$$

$$\angle z = 61.5°$$

Calculator:

$$180 \ \boxed{-} \ 57 \ \boxed{=} \ 123 \ \boxed{\div} \ 2 \ \boxed{=} \ 61.5$$

Since $\overline{EG} \parallel \overline{DF}$ then $\angle x = \angle z = 61.5°$

12.   **(B)**

$$\vec{A} + \vec{B} = [2 + (-1)] + (3 + 2)i$$

$$= 1 + 5i$$

13.   **(D)**

Perpendicular lines have slopes which are negative reciprocals of each other. To find the coordinates of point B, use the equation for the line CB.

$$y - y_1 = m(x - x_1)$$

with m_{CB} = slope of CB,

$(x_1, y_1) = (3, 5)$,

and $m_{CB} = \dfrac{-1}{m_{AC}}$.

$m_{AC} = \dfrac{5-2}{3-1} = \dfrac{3}{2}$

$m_{CB} = \dfrac{-1}{\dfrac{3}{2}}$

Calculator:

$$\boxed{()}\ \boxed{()}\ 5\ \boxed{-}\ 2\ \boxed{()}\ \boxed{\div}\ \boxed{()}\ 3\ \boxed{-}\ 1\ \boxed{()}\ \boxed{()}\ 3\ \boxed{\div}\ 2\ \boxed{=}\ \boxed{1/x} = -0.67$$

Then using

$$y - y_1 = m_{CB}(x - x_1)$$

solve for x.

$$x = \dfrac{y - y_1}{m_{CB}} + x_1$$

$$= \dfrac{-6}{-0.67} + 3$$

Calculator:

$$1\ \boxed{+/-}\ \boxed{+}\ 5\ \boxed{+/-}\ \boxed{=}\ -6\ \boxed{\div}\ .67\ \boxed{+/-}\ \boxed{=}\ 9\ \boxed{+}\ 3\ \boxed{=}\ 12$$

14.   **(C)**

There are $4 + 6 + 3 + 8 = 21$ balls in total. Of these 21 balls, $12\ (= 4 + 8)$ are either white or green.

Hence the probability is 12 in 21 or $\dfrac{12}{21} = \dfrac{4}{7}$ that the ball we pick is white or green.

15.   **(E)**

First, find the probability of picking the red ball.

$$\text{prob (red ball)} = \dfrac{\#\ \text{red balls}}{\text{total}} = \dfrac{15}{30 + 40 + 15}$$

Calculator:

$$15 \;\boxed{\div}\; \boxed{()}\; 30 \;\boxed{+}\; 40 \;\boxed{+}\; 15 \;\boxed{()}\; \boxed{=}\; 0.1765$$

For the second pick,

$$\text{prob (yellow ball)} = \frac{\text{\# yellow balls}}{\text{total}} = \frac{30}{30+40+15}$$

Calculator:

$$30 \;\boxed{\div}\; \boxed{()}\; 30 \;\boxed{+}\; 40 \;\boxed{+}\; 14 \;\boxed{()}\; \boxed{=}\; 0.3571$$

prob (red) × prob (yellow) = $0.1765 \times 0.3571 = 0.0630$

16. **(B)**

The general equation of a parabola with vertex at the origin and symmetrical about the y-axis is

$$y = ax^2 .$$

Use the point $(1, 2)$ to find a.

$$2 = a(1)^2$$

$$a = 2$$

Therefore, the equation should be $y = 2x^2$.

17. **(A)**

$f(\text{domain}) = \text{range}$

$f(0) = 0^2 + 2 \times 0 - 5 = -5$

$f(1) = 1^2 + 2 \times 1 - 5 = -3$

$f(2) = 2^2 + 2 \times 2 - 5 = 3$

$f(3) = 3^2 + 2 \times 3 - 5 = 10$

The range is $\{-5, -3, 3, 10\}$. Therefore, choice (A) is not in the range.

18. **(B)**

All radii of the circle are equal, so each triangle is isosceles. Therefore, all internal angles must equal 60°.

19. **(D)**

$3 \;⊕\; (-2) = 2(3)(-2) + (-2)$

$$= -12 + (-2)$$

$$= -14$$

20.　　**(C)**

The area of the shape is the area of the larger rectangle minus the area of the smaller rectangle. (See figure.)

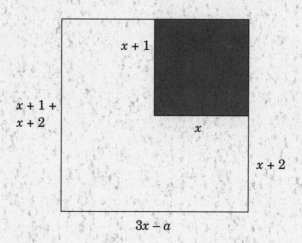

$$(x + 1 + x + 2)(3x - a) - (x + 1)x = 150$$

Substitute for the value of x, and solve for a.

$$(4.5 + 1 + 4.5 + 2)(3(4.5) - a) - (4.5 + 1)(4.5) = 150$$

$$12(13.5 - a) - 5.5(4.5) = 150$$

$$a = 13.5 - \frac{150 + 24.75}{12}$$

Calculator:

150 ⊞ 24.75 ⊟ 174.75 ⊡ 12 ⊟ 14.56

13.5 ⊟ 14.56 ⊟ −1.06

21.　　**(E)**

Rearrange into quadratic form:

$$2m^2 - 3m - 1 = 0$$

$$am^2 + bm + c = 0$$

then use the quadratic formula:

$$x = \frac{-b \pm \sqrt{b^2 - 4ac}}{2a}$$

substituting $a = 2$, $b = -3$, and $c = -1$,

$$x = \frac{-(-3) \pm \sqrt{(-3)^2 - 4\,(2)\,(1)}}{2\,(2)}$$

Evaluate the $\boxed{\sqrt{}}$ term

Calculator:

$$3 \boxed{+/-} \boxed{x^2} \boxed{-} 4 \boxed{\times} 2 \boxed{\times} 1 \boxed{+/-} \boxed{=} 17 \boxed{\sqrt{}} = 4.12$$

$$x = \frac{3 + 4.12}{4} = 1.78$$

$$x = \frac{3 - 4.12}{4} = -0.28$$

22.   (A)

The equation of the line passing through (1, 2) and (3, 4) is obtained from the point-slope equation:

$$\frac{y - y_1}{x - x_1} = m \qquad m \text{ is the slope}$$

Let $(x, y) = (1, 2)$ and $(x_1, y_1) = (3, 4)$:

$$m = \frac{2 - 4}{1 - 3} = \frac{-2}{-2} = 1$$

Thus, the slope is 1.

The equation of the line is thus

$$\frac{y - 4}{x - 3} = 1 \qquad \text{or}$$

$$y - 4 = x - 3 \quad \text{or}$$

$$x - y + 1 = 0$$

Thus, the x-intercept is obtained by setting $y = 0$.

$$x - 0 + 1 = 0$$

Therefore, $x = -1$ is the x-intercept.

23.   (B)

Since $CD \parallel AB$, $\triangle CED \approx \triangle AEB$. If two triangles are similar, then the ratio of their areas is equal to the square of the ratio of their sides. Therefore,

$$\frac{\text{Area of } \triangle CED}{\text{Area of } \triangle AEB} = \left(\frac{CD}{AB}\right)^2 = \left(\frac{1}{2}\right)^2 = \frac{1}{4}$$

24.   **(B)**

The volume of the shaded area is the volume of the rectangular solid minus the volume of the sphere.

$$\text{shaded volume} = \text{rectangular volume} - \text{sphere volume}$$

$$= lwh - \frac{4}{3}\pi r^3$$

$$= 3.27 \times 1.45 \times 1.45 - \frac{4}{3}\pi(0.73)^3$$

Calculator:

3.27 ☒ 1.45 ☒ 1.45 ☐ 6.88 ☐ ⬭ 4 ÷ 3 ⬭ ☒ π ☒ ⬭ .73
y^x 3 ⬭ ☐ 5.25

25.   **(D)**

$$f(g(5)) = f\left(\frac{1}{3\,(5)}\right)$$

$$= f\left(\frac{1}{15}\right)$$

$$= 2\left(\frac{1}{15}\right) + 3$$

$$= 3\frac{2}{15}$$

26.   **(E)**

$2\cos^2\theta + 2\sin^2\theta$

$$= 2(\cos^2\theta + \sin^2\theta) \qquad (\text{Because } \cos^2\theta + \sin^2\theta = 1)$$

$$= 2$$

27.   **(C)**

Calculate the mean, median, and mode.

$$\text{Mean} = \frac{72 + 75 + 83 + 83 + 86 + 92 + 97}{7} = 84$$

Median is the middle number of the group after ranking; therefore, 83 is the median.

The mode is the number that appears the most frequently. Eighty-three appears twice; all others appear once; therefore, 83 is the mode.

28. **(E)**

$$\tan\beta = \frac{\text{opposite side}}{\text{adjacent side}}$$

By the Pythagorean theorem:

$$a = \sqrt{c^2 - b^2}$$

$$= \sqrt{22.2^2 - 13^2}$$

Calculator:

22.2 $\boxed{x^2}$ -13 $\boxed{x^2}$ $\boxed{=}$ 324 $\boxed{\sqrt{}}$ $\boxed{=}$ 18

$$\tan\beta = \frac{13}{18} = 0.7222$$

Calculator:

13 $\boxed{\div}$ 18 $\boxed{=}$ 0.7222

29. **(E)**

$$g(f(x)) = \sqrt{\frac{x^3 - 5x + 9}{25x^4}}$$

$$g(f(4)) = \sqrt{\frac{4^3 - 5\,(4) + 9}{25\,(4)^4}}$$

Calculator:

4 $\boxed{y^x}$ 3 $\boxed{-}$ 5 $\boxed{\times}$ 4 $\boxed{+}$ 9 $\boxed{=}$ 53 $\boxed{\div}$ $\boxed{(\,)}$ 25 $\boxed{\times}$ 4 $\boxed{y^x}$ $\boxed{(\,)}$ $\boxed{=}$ 0.0083 $\boxed{\sqrt{}}$ $=$ 0.091

30. **(B)**

$$(2^{4x})(8^{2x}) = (2^{4x})(2^3)^{2x}$$

$$= (2^{4x})(2^{6x})$$

$$= 2^{4x+6x}$$

$$= 2^{10x}$$

31.   **(D)**

$$y = 2(x-3)^2$$

$$= 2(-1-3)^2$$

$$= 2(-4)^2$$

$$= 32$$

32.   **(B)**

$$b - 2 = 3$$

$$b = 5$$

$$ab - 3 = 7$$

$$5a - 3 = 7$$

$$5a = 10$$

$$a = 2$$

33.   **(B)**

Slope = 2 and y-intercept = 1.

34.   **(A)**

The cost of one pen and one pencil = $\dfrac{\$16.20}{12}$ = \$1.35.

The cost of one pen = \$1.35 − \$0.15 = \$1.20.

35.   **(C)**

Surface area = $4\pi r^2$

$$= 4\pi \left(\frac{d}{2}\right)^2$$

$$= 4\pi \left(\frac{10}{2}\right)^2$$

$$= 100\pi$$

36.   **(B)**

$$\begin{cases} x + 2y = 5 & (1) \\ 2x + 3y = 2 & (2) \end{cases}$$

Multiply equation (1) by 2 and subtract equation (2):

$$2x + 4y = 10$$
$$-(2x + 3y = 2)$$
$$\overline{4 = 8}$$

Substitute $y = 8$ into (1):

$$x + 2\,(8) = 5$$

$$x = -11$$

Therefore, $(-11, 8)$ is the intersection point of the given pair of lines.

37.   **(B)**

$$\sin \alpha = \frac{\text{opposite side}}{\text{hypotenuse}} = \frac{7}{a} = 0.8965$$

Calculator:

$$63.7 \; \boxed{\sin} \; = 0.8965$$

$$a = \frac{7}{0.8965} = 7.81$$

Calculator:

$$7 \; \boxed{\div} \; 0.8965 \; \boxed{=} \; 7.81$$

38.   **(A)**

Parallel lines have equal slopes.

Slope of the line $3x - 4y = 12$:

$$3x - 4y = 12$$

$$4y = 3x - 12$$

$$y = \frac{3}{4}x - 3$$

$$\text{Slope} = \frac{3}{4}$$

Thus, the slope of $Ax + 6y = -9$ is $\dfrac{3}{4}$.

Slope of the line $Ax + 6y = -9$:

$$Ax + 6y = -9$$

$$6y = -Ax - 9$$

$$y = -\frac{A}{6}x - \frac{3}{2}$$

Hence,

$$-\frac{A}{6} = \frac{3}{4}$$

$$A = \frac{-18}{4}$$

$$= \frac{-9}{2}$$

39.   **(B)**

$$2x + 5 > 11$$

$$2x > 6$$

$$x > 3$$

40.   **(C)**

$$ab = (3 + 2i)\,(1 + 4i)$$

$$= 3 + 12i + 2i + 8i^2$$

$$= (3 - 8) + 14i$$

$$= -5 + 14i$$

41.   **(D)**

$\triangle ACB$ is isosceles because $AC = CD = BC$. Then,

$$\angle ABC = \frac{1}{2}(70°) = 35°$$

$$\angle BCA = 180° - 70° = 110°$$
$$\theta = 110° + 35° = 145°$$

42.   **(A)**

Let x be the liters of solution B needed; thus $10 - x$ is the number of liters of solution A.

$$0.30\ (10 - x) + 0.65x = 0.46 \times 10$$

Solving for x:

$$3 - 0.3x + 0.65x = 4.6$$

$$x(-0.3 + 0.65) = 4.6 - 3$$

$$x = \frac{4.6 - 3}{0.65 - 0.3}$$

$$= 4.57$$

43.   **(D)**

$$a^2 b^3 = 3^7$$

$$9^2 b^3 = 3^7$$

$$3^4 b^3 = 3^7$$

$$b^3 = 3^3$$

$$b = 3$$

44.   **(B)**

The die has six sides and thus the probability of getting any side is $\frac{1}{6}$.

The probability of getting two sides is $\frac{2}{6}$. Getting either a 4 or a 5 is $\frac{2}{6} = 0.3333$.

45.   **(A)**

$$y = f(x + 3)$$

$$= 3(x + 3) + 4$$

$$= 3x + 9 + 4$$

$$= 3x + 13$$

Therefore, the slope of the line is 3.

46.   **(B)**

The line passes through (−1, 2) and (0, 3).

$$\frac{y-3}{x-0} = \frac{3-2}{0-(-1)}$$

$$y - 3 = x$$

$$y = x + 3$$

47.   **(A)**

$$(3 + 2i)(1 + 3i) = 3 + 9i + 2i + 6i^2$$

$$= -3 + 11i$$

Therefore, $x = -3$.

48.   **(C)**

$$(x + 1)(x^2 + 4x - 5) = 0$$

$$x = -1 \text{ or } \quad x^2 + 4x - 5 = 0$$

$$(x + 5)(x - 1) = 0$$

$$x = -5 \text{ or } x = 1$$

Therefore, −5, −1, and 1 are the roots of the equation.

49.   **(C)**

Given points $R(x_1, y_1)$ and $S(x_2, y_2)$, the coordinates of the midpoint are:

$$U(x, y) = \left(\frac{x_1 + x_2}{2}, \frac{y_1 + y_2}{2} \right)$$

$$= \left(\frac{1.14 + 3.78}{2}, \frac{2.78 + 0.89}{2} \right)$$

$$x = 2.46$$
$$y = 1.84$$

50.　　**(C)**

$$\frac{3}{x+2} = \frac{5}{x+7}$$

$$3x + 21 = 5x + 10$$

$$11 = 2x$$

$$x = \frac{11}{2}$$

THE SAT SUBJECT TEST IN

Math
Level 1

PRACTICE TEST 5

SAT Mathematics
Level 1

Practice Test 5

Time: 1 Hour
50 Questions

DIRECTIONS: Choose the best answer for each question and mark the letter of your selection on the corresponding answer sheet.

NOTES:

(1) Some questions require the use of a calculator. You must decide when the use of your calculator will be helpful.

(2) Make sure your calculator is in degree mode.

(3) All figures are drawn to scale and lie in a plane unless otherwise stated.

(4) The domain of any function f is the set of all real numbers x for which $f(x)$ is a real number, unless other information is provided.

REFERENCE INFORMATION: The following information may be helpful in answering some of the questions.

Volume of a right circular cone with radius r and height h	$V = \dfrac{1}{3}\pi r^2 h$
Lateral area of a right circular cone with circumference c and slant height l	$S = \dfrac{1}{2}cl$
Volume of a sphere with radius r	$V = \dfrac{4}{3}\pi r^3$
Surface area of a sphere with radius r	$S = 4\pi r^2$
Volume of a pyramid with base area B and height h	$V = \dfrac{1}{3}Bh$

1. Solve for x.

   $$|27x - 540| < |36x + 1,440|$$

   (A) $x = -14.3$

   (B) $-14.2 < x < 14.3$

   (C) $x > -14.3, x < -220$

   (D) $x < -14.3$

   (E) No solution

2. If $|2x - 5| = 3$, then

   (A) $x = -2\frac{1}{2}$ or 3.

   (B) $x = 2\frac{1}{2}$ or 4.

   (C) $x = 1$ or 3.

   (D) $x = 1$ or 4.

   (E) $x = 0$ or -3.

3. If $\frac{2}{3}x = 0$, then $\frac{2}{3} + x =$

   (A) $\frac{4}{9}$.

   (B) $\frac{2}{3}$.

   (C) 1.

   (D) $\frac{4}{3}$.

   (E) 2.

4. If $\frac{x}{y} = \frac{2}{5}$, then $25x^2 - 4y^2 =$

   (A) -5.

   (B) -2.

   (C) 0.

   (D) 2.

   (E) 5.

5.

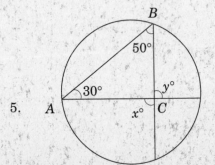

In the figure on the previous page, two chords of the circle intersect, making the angles shown. What is the value of $x + y$?

(A) 40°

(D) 160°

(B) 50°

(E) 320°

(C) 80°

6.   If $\dfrac{3}{a+2} = \dfrac{5}{a+4}$, then $a =$

(A) $\dfrac{1}{2}$.

(D) $\dfrac{3}{2}$.

(B) 1.

(E) 2.

(C) $\dfrac{5}{4}$.

7.   Determine the roots of $15x^2 + 30x - 60$.

(A) (−3.236, 1.236)

(D) (−30, 30)

(B) (−1.236, 3.236)

(E) No real roots

(C) (−2, 2)

8.   Evaluate: $\sqrt{1 - \cos^2(60°)}$.

(A) 0.5

(D) −0.866

(B) −0.5

(E) Undefined

(C) 0.866

9. $2\dfrac{1}{2}$ 3

A   B   C   D

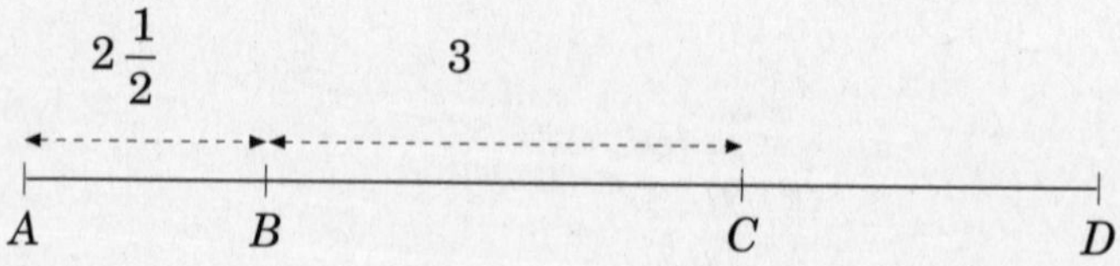

In figure above, if $\dfrac{AB}{BD} = \dfrac{1}{2}$, then the length of CD is

(A) $\dfrac{1}{2}$.

(D) $2\dfrac{3}{4}$.

(B) 2.

(E) 3.

(C) $2\dfrac{1}{2}$.

10. What is the equation of a line which passes through the point $(-1,2)$ and perpendicular to a line whose equation is given by $x - 3y + 2 = 0$?

(A) $x - 3y + 1 = 0$

(D) $3x + y - 1 = 0$

(B) $x - 3y = 0$

(E) $3x + y + 1 = 0$

(C) $3x + y - 2 = 0$

11. If an operation $*$ is defined for all real numbers a and b by the equation $a * b = a + b - ab$, then $5 * (-2) =$

(A) -10.

(D) 7.

(B) 0.

(E) 13.

(C) 3.

12. $(F \times G)(x)$ is defined as $F(G(x))$; evaluate $(F \times G)(x)$ if $G(x) = 12x - 15$ and $F(x) = \left(\dfrac{2}{3}\right)x + 2$, where $x = 2$.

(A) 9

(D) $\dfrac{10}{3}$

(B) 2

(E) 25

(C) 8

For problems 13, 14, and 15, refer to the cube with side-length of 5 units, with the inscribed sphere.

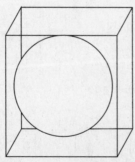

13. Determine the volume of the sphere.

    (A) 78.54 sq. units

    (B) 78.54 cubic units

    (C) 26.18 cubic units

    (D) 523.6 cubic units

    (E) 65.45 cubic units

14. Determine the surface area of the cube and the sphere.

    (A) 228.54 sq. units

    (B) 125 sq. units

    (C) 46.46 sq. units

    (D) 314.16 sq. units

    (E) 203.54 sq. units

15. Determine the volume between the sphere and the cube.

    (A) 125 cubic units

    (B) 59.55 cubic units

    (C) 398.6 cubic units

    (D) 46.46 sq. units

    (E) 9.29 sq. units

For problems 16 and 17, refer to the picture below

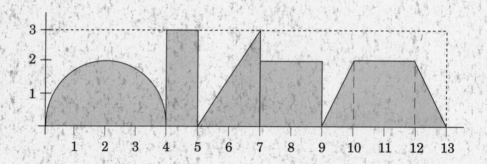

16. Find the total area of the shaded regions in the above diagram.

    (A) 22.28 sq. units

    (B) 22.28 + 2(π) sq. units

    (C) 25.28 sq. units

    (D) 28.57 sq. units

    (E) 18.57 sq. units

17. Find the area of the unshaded region of the dotted rectangle.

    (A) 22.28 sq. units

    (B) 39 sq. units

    (C) 16.72 sq. units

    (D) 5.56 sq. units

    (E) 28.57 sq. units

18. If $i^2 = -1$ and $x = 2 + 5i$, then $\dfrac{1}{x} =$

(A) $\dfrac{2}{27} + \dfrac{5}{27}i$.

(D) $2 + 5i$.

(B) $\dfrac{2}{29} - \dfrac{5}{29}i$.

(E) $3 + 10i$.

(C) $\dfrac{1}{2} + \dfrac{1}{5}i$.

19. What is the y-intercept of the equation $y = |x - 5|$?

(A) −5

(D) 3

(B) −2

(E) 5

(C) 0

20. Evaluate $2\cos(\theta)\sin(\theta)$ when $\theta = 15$.

(A) 1.9318

(D) −0.2588

(B) 0.2588

(E) −0.5

(C) 0.5

21. Which of the following is not the graph of a function of x?

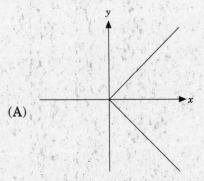
(A)

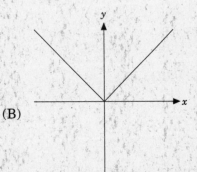
(B)

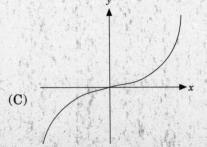
(C)

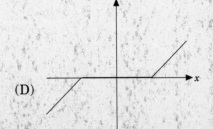
(D)

(E)

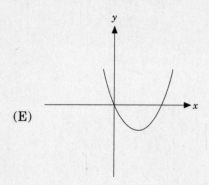

22. If $abc \neq 0$, then $\dfrac{25\left(\dfrac{a}{b}\right)^3\left(\dfrac{c}{a}\right)^4}{125\left(\dfrac{a}{c}\right)^7\left(\dfrac{b}{c}\right)^{-2}} =$

(A) $\dfrac{a^8 b}{5c^9}$.

(D) $\dfrac{c^6}{5a^2 b^4}$.

(B) $\dfrac{c^9}{5a^8 b}$.

(E) $\dfrac{c^{10}}{5ab^5}$.

(C) $\dfrac{c^7}{25a^7 b^2}$.

23. Solve for x when $x = -4$.
$6x^3 - 29x + 35$

(A) 15

(D) -303

(B) -233

(E) -465

(C) 343

24. Given the parabola $y = x^2 + 1$ with line $y = 10$ below, the total restricted area of the parabola is 36 sq. units. What is the area of the shaded region?

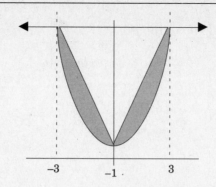

(A)   15 sq. units   (D)   4.5 sq. units

(B)   9 sq. units   (E)   −18 sq. units

(C)   27 sq. units

25. A class has 4 quizzes worth 30% (w1) of their grade, 3 tests worth 40% (w2), and a final worth 30% (w3). If these are Jenny's scores, what will her grade-point average be?

quizzes: 67, 75, 85, and 72

tests: 85, 95, and 80

final: 83

(A)   87.12%   (D)   80.25%

(B)   77.12%   (E)   82%

(C)   81.47%

For problems 26 and 27, refer to the graph below.

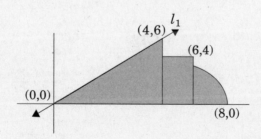

26. Determine the slope of line l_1.

(A) $-\dfrac{2}{3}$

(D) $\dfrac{2}{3}$

(B) 4

(E) $-\dfrac{3}{2}$

(C) $\dfrac{3}{2}$

27. Determine the area of the shaded region.

(A) 35. 14 sq. units

(D) 29.14 sq. units

(B) 19.14 sq. units

(E) 23.14 sq. units

(C) 20 sq. units

28. A sphere with diameter 1 meter has a mass of 120 kilograms. What is the mass, in kilograms, of a sphere of the same kind of material that has a diameter of 2 meters?

(A) 480

(D) 960

(B) 560

(E) 1,080

(C) 640

29. If $f(x) = \dfrac{x}{5} - 3$ and the domain is the interval $-5 < x < 15$, then the range of $f(x)$ is

(A) $-5 < f(x) < 15.$

(D) $-3 < f(x) < 3.$

(B) $0 < f(x) < 10.$

(E) $-4 < f(x) < 0.$

(C) $-5 < f(x) < 7.$

30. If θ is an acute angle and $\cos\theta = \dfrac{x}{y}$, where $x > 0$, $y > 0$, and $x \neq y$, $\tan\theta =$

(A) $\dfrac{y}{\sqrt{x^2 + y^2}}.$

(D) $\dfrac{\sqrt{x^2 - y^2}}{y}.$

(B) $\dfrac{\sqrt{y^2 - x^2}}{\sqrt{x^2 - y^2}}.$

(E) $\dfrac{\sqrt{x^2 + y^2}}{xy}.$

(C) $\dfrac{\sqrt{y^2 - x^2}}{x}.$

31. What is the probability of getting at most one head in three coin tosses?

(A) 0

(D) $\frac{3}{4}$

(B) $\frac{1}{4}$

(E) $\frac{7}{8}$

(C) $\frac{1}{2}$

32.

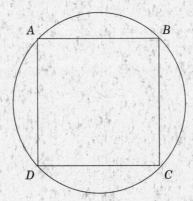

In the figure above, if square $ABCD$ has a side of length 3, then the circumference of the circumscribed circle is

(A) 12π

(D) $6\pi \sqrt{2}$

(B) $4\pi \sqrt{3}$

(E) $3\pi \sqrt{2}$

(C) $2\pi \sqrt{10}$

33. What is the equation of a parabola which is symmetrical about the y-axis and passes through points $(0, -2)$ and $(2, 0)$?

(A) $y = x^2 - 2$

(D) $y = 2x^2 - 1$

(B) $y = \frac{1}{2}x^2 - 2$

(E) $y = 2x^2 - \frac{1}{2}$

(C) $y = \frac{3}{2}x^2 + \frac{1}{2}$

34.

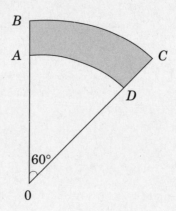

In the above figure, *AOD* and *BOC* are sectors of concentric circles.

If *OA* = 7 and *AB* = 2, then the area of the shaded region is

(A) π.

(D) $\dfrac{13}{3}\pi$.

(B) 2π.

(E) $\dfrac{16}{3}\pi$.

(C) $\dfrac{7}{2}\pi$.

35. If $x^2 - 3x - 4 < 0$, then the solution set is

(A) $-4 < x < 1$.

(D) $-1 < x < 0$.

(B) $-4 < x < -3$.

(E) $-1 < x < 4$.

(C) $-3 < x < 0$.

36. If the cost of five apples is $3.25, and if the cost of an orange and one of these apples together is $1.05, what is the cost of an orange alone?

(A) $0.35

(D) $0.50

(B) $0.40

(E) $0.55

(C) $0.45

37.

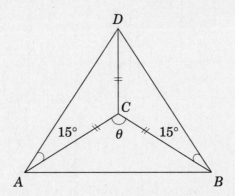

In the figure above, if $AC = BC = CD$ and $\angle CAD = \angle CBD = 15°$ then $\theta =$

(A) 15°.

(D) 60°.

(B) 30°.

(E) 75°.

(C) 45°.

38. What is the least positive integer x for which $5 - x$ and $11 - x$ will be non-zero and have opposite signs?

(A) 0

(D) –8

(B) 5

(E) –11

(C) 6

39. The law of refraction states that $n_1 \sin\theta_1 = n_2 \sin\theta_2$ where n is the index of refraction for the material and θ is the angle of a light ray with the vertical to the material. Determine the angle of the light ray from air to glass if $(\theta_1) = 30$ and $n_{glass} = 1.517$.

(A) 0.3297

(D) 19.25

(B) 3.035

(E) 49.35

(C) 15

40. What is the area of an equilateral triangle with perimeter equal to $7\frac{1}{2}$?

(A) $\dfrac{3}{2}$

(D) $\dfrac{25\sqrt{3}}{9}$

(B) $\dfrac{3\sqrt{3}}{2}$

(E) $\dfrac{5\sqrt{3}}{4}$

(C) $\dfrac{25\sqrt{3}}{16}$

41. Which of the following is the graph of the equation $y = 2x + 1$?

(A)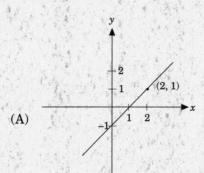

(B)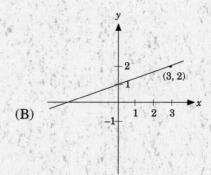

(C)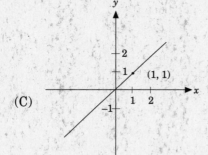

(D)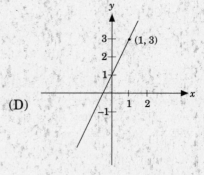

(E)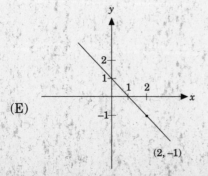

42.

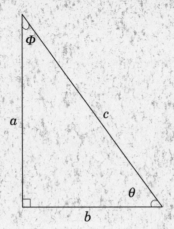

In the right triangle in the figure above, $\tan\theta$ is equal to which of the following?

I. $\dfrac{\sin\theta}{\cos\theta}$

II. $\dfrac{\cos\Phi}{\sin\Phi}$

III. $\dfrac{a}{b}$

(A) I only

(B) II only

(C) III only

(D) I and II only

(E) I, II, and III

43. Which of the following inequalities has a solution set on the real axis?

(A) $x^2 < -1$

(B) $x^2 + 2x + 2 > 0$

(C) $-3x^2 + x - 1 > 0$

(D) $x^2 < -4$

(E) None of the above

44. The coordinates of the point of intersection of the lines having equations $3x + 2y = 5$ and $x - 4y = 1$ are

    (A) $\left(-\dfrac{11}{7}, -\dfrac{1}{7}\right).$

    (B) $\left(-\dfrac{11}{7}, -\dfrac{2}{7}\right).$

    (C) $\left(\dfrac{11}{7}, \dfrac{1}{7}\right).$

    (D) $\left(\dfrac{11}{7}, \dfrac{2}{7}\right).$

    (E) $\left(\dfrac{11}{7}, \dfrac{16}{7}\right).$

45. If $c = 18a + 24b$ where a and b are positive integers, then c must be divisible by which of the following?

    (A) 4

    (B) 6

    (C) 9

    (D) 12

    (E) 72

46. The following instructions are executed by a computer.

    1. LET SUM = 0

    2. LET N = 1

    3. IF N < = 5 GO TO INSTRUCTION 4 OTHERWISE GO TO INSTRUCTION 7

    4. LET SUM = SUM + N

    5. LET N = N + 1

    6. GO TO INSTRUCTION 3

    7. WRITE THE FINAL VALUE OF SUM.

    What is the final value of SUM?

    (A) 5

    (B) 10

    (C) 15

    (D) 21

    (E) 25

47. If x is an odd integer and y is even, then which of the following must be an even integer?

I. $2x + 3y$

II. xy

III. $x + y - 1$

(A) I only.

(B) II only.

(C) I and II only.

(D) II and III only.

(E) I, II, and III.

48. If $0° \leq \theta \leq 45°$ and $\sin 2\theta = \dfrac{\sqrt{3}}{2}$, then $(\cos\theta + \sin\theta)^2 =$

(A) $1 - \dfrac{\sqrt{3}}{2}$.

(B) 1.

(C) $1 + \dfrac{\sqrt{3}}{2}$.

(D) $1 + \sqrt{3}$.

(E) $1 + 2\sqrt{3}$.

49. Which shaded region is larger and by how much?

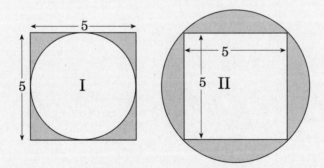

(A) II by 8.893 sq. units

(B) I by 5.365 sq. units

(C) II by 14.258 sq. units

(D) I by 5π sq. units

(E) The areas are equal.

50.

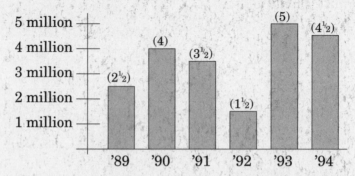

Given the above graph of the income for a company over six years, what is the mean (average) income for all six years?

(A) 4 million

(B) 3.5 million

(C) 1.5 million

(D) 3.75 million

(E) 2.5 million

TEST 5

ANSWER KEY

1. (C)	14. (A)	27. (E)	40. (C)
2. (D)	15. (B)	28. (D)	41. (D)
3. (B)	16. (A)	29. (E)	42. (E)
4. (C)	17. (C)	30. (C)	43. (E)
5. (D)	18. (B)	31. (C)	44. (C)
6. (B)	19. (E)	32. (E)	45. (B)
7. (A)	20. (C)	33. (B)	46. (C)
8. (C)	21. (A)	34. (E)	47. (E)
9. (B)	22. (B)	35. (E)	48. (C)
10. (E)	23. (B)	36. (B)	49. (A)
11. (E)	24. (B)	37. (D)	50. (B)
12. (C)	25. (E)	38. (C)	
13. (E)	26. (C)	39. (D)	

DETAILED EXPLANATIONS
OF ANSWERS

1. **(C)**

$$27x - 540 > -(36x + 1440)$$
$$63x > -900$$

Calculator:

$$900 \;\boxed{+/-}\; \boxed{\div}\; 63 \;\boxed{=}\; -14.285$$

$$x > -14.285$$

Compute:

$$27x - 540 = (36x + 1440)$$
$$x = -220$$

Test a value < -220

And a value > -220

$$x < -220$$

2. **(D)**

$$|2x - 5| = 3$$

$$2x - 5 = 3 \qquad\qquad 2x - 5 = -3$$
$$2x = 8 \qquad\qquad\quad 2x = 2$$
$$x = 4 \qquad\qquad\quad x = 1$$

Therefore, $x = 1$ or 4 is the solution to the given equation.

3. **(B)**

$$\frac{2}{3}x = 0 \Rightarrow x = 0$$

Therefore, $\dfrac{2}{3} + x = \dfrac{2}{3}$

4. **(C)**

$$\frac{x}{y} = \frac{2}{5}$$

$$x = \frac{2}{5}y$$

Substitute $x = \dfrac{2}{5}y$ into the equation:

$$25\left(\frac{2}{5}y\right)^2 - 4y^2$$

$$= 25\left(\frac{4y^2}{25}\right) - 4y^2$$

$$= 4y^2 - 4y^2 = 0$$

5.   **(D)**

$x = \angle CBA + \angle CAB$

$\quad = 50° + 30°$

$\quad = 80°$

$x = y$ (vertically opposite angles)

Therefore, $x + y = 2(80°) = 160°$.

6.   **(B)**

$$\frac{3}{a+2} = \frac{5}{a+4} \qquad \text{(cross multiply)}$$

$$3(a+4) = 5(a+2)$$

$$3a + 12 = 5a + 10$$

$$2a = 2$$

$$a = 1$$

7.   **(A)**

By the quadratic formula

$$\frac{-30 \pm \sqrt{(30)^2 - 4(15)(-60)}}{2(15)}$$

Calculator:

$30 \;\boxed{x^2}\; \boxed{-}\; 4 \;\boxed{\times}\; 15 \;\boxed{\times}\; 60 \;\boxed{+/-}\; \boxed{=}\; 4500$

$$\frac{-30 \pm \sqrt{4,500}}{30}$$

Calculator:

$4500 \;\boxed{\sqrt{\;}}\; = 67.082$

$$\frac{-30 \pm 67.082}{30}$$

Calculator:

30 +/− + 67.082 = ÷ 30 = 1.236

30 +/− − 67.082 = ÷ 30 = −3.236

(−3.236, 1.236)

8.   **(C)**

$$\sqrt{1-(0.5)^2}$$

$$\sqrt{1-(0.25)}$$ $$\sqrt{1-\cos^2(60°)} = \sin(60°)$$

$$\sqrt{0.75} = 0.866$$ $$= 0.866$$

Calculator:

1 − 60 cos x^2 = $\sqrt{}$ = 0.866

9.   **(B)**

$$\frac{AB}{BD} = \frac{1}{2}$$

$$BD = 2AB$$

$$BD = 2\left(2\frac{1}{2}\right)$$

$$BD = 5$$

$$CD = BD - BC$$

$$= 5 - 3$$

$$= 2$$

10.   **(E)**

If two lines are perpendicular, the slope of one line is the negative reciprocal of the other. We can rewrite the equation of the line given so that it appears in slope intercept form. That is

$$x - 3y + 2 = 0$$

$$x + 2 = 3y$$

$$\frac{1}{3}x + \frac{2}{3} = y$$

In this form, the coefficient of the x variable is the slope of the given line. Therefore, the slope of the line which is perpendicular to it is -3.

Since we know of a point on the line and the slope of the line, the obvious choice for the form of the equation is the point-slope form: $y - y_0 = m(x - x_0)$, where m is the slope and (x_0, y_0) is the given point.

Substituting yields: $y - 2 = -3(x - (-1))$

$$y - 2 = -3x - 3$$

$$y = -3x - 1.$$

Adding $3x + 1$ on both sides we obtain

$$3x + y + 1 = 0.$$

11.

Substitute $a = 5$ and $b = -2$ into the given expression.

$$5 * (-2) = 5 + (-2) - 5(-2)$$

$$= 5 - 2 + 10$$

$$= 13$$

12.

$$(FG)(x) = F(G(x)) = F(12x - 15) = \left(\frac{2}{3}\right)(12x - 15) + 8 =$$

$$8x - 10 + 2 =$$

$$8 \times 2 - 8 = 8$$

You could also substitute 2 in $G(x)$ to get a number and then put that number in $F(x)$ for the same result.

13.

$V = \left(\frac{4}{3}\right)\pi r^3$ where the radius is 2.5 units $V = \left(\frac{4}{3}\right)\pi(2.5)^3 = 65.45$ cubic units.

Calculator:

$\boxed{\pi}$ $\boxed{\times}$ 2.5 $\boxed{y^x}$ 3 $\boxed{\times}$ 4 $\boxed{\div}$ 3 $\boxed{=}$ 65.45

14. **(A)**

Surface area $= 6(s)^2 + 4\pi r^2$
$$= 6(5)^2 + 4\pi\,2.5^2$$

Calculator:

$\boxed{\pi}$ $\boxed{\times}$ 4 $\boxed{\times}$ 2.5 $\boxed{x^2}$ $\boxed{+}$ 6 $\boxed{\times}$ 5 $\boxed{x^2}$ $\boxed{=}$ 228.539 sq. units

15. **(B)**

$$v = s^3 - \left(\frac{4}{3}\right)r^3$$

$$= 5^3 - \left(\frac{4}{3}\right)2.5^3$$

Calculator:

5 $\boxed{y^x}$ 3 $\boxed{-}$ 4 $\boxed{\times}$ $\boxed{\pi}$ $\boxed{\times}$ 2.5 $\boxed{y^x}$ 3 $\boxed{\div}$ 3 $\boxed{=}$ 59.55

59.55 cubic units

16. **(A)**

$$A = \left(\frac{1}{2}\right)\pi 2^2 + (1)(3) + \left(\frac{1}{2}\right)2(3) + 2(2) + \left(\frac{1}{2}\right)(2)(4+2)$$

$A = 2\pi + 16 = 22.28$ sq. units

Calculator:

.5 $\boxed{\times}$ $\boxed{\pi}$ $\boxed{\times}$ 2 $\boxed{x^2}$ $\boxed{+}$ 3 $\boxed{+}$ .5 $\boxed{\times}$ 6 $\boxed{+}$ 4 $\boxed{+}$ 6 $\boxed{=}$ 22.28

17. **(C)**

Area $=$ area of rectangle $-$ area from 16
$$= 3(13) - 22.28 = 16.72 \text{ sq. units}$$

Calculator:

3 $\boxed{\times}$ 13 $\boxed{-}$ 22.28 $\boxed{=}$ 16.72

18. **(B)**

$$\frac{1}{2+5i} = \frac{1}{2+5i} \times \frac{2-5i}{2-5i}$$

$$= \frac{2-5i}{2^2 - 25i^2}$$

$$= \frac{2-5i}{4+25}$$

$$= \frac{2-5i}{29}$$

$$= \frac{2}{29} - \frac{5}{29}i.$$

19. **(E)**

Substitute $x = 0$ into the given equation.

$$y = |0 - 5|$$

$$= 5$$

20. **(C)**

$$2\cos 15° \sin 15° = 2(0.9659)(0.2588)$$

$$= 0.5$$

Calculator:

$2 \boxed{\times} 15 \boxed{\cos} \boxed{\times} 15 \boxed{\sin} \boxed{=} 0.5$

21. **(A)**

When x is positive, there will be two corresponding values of y. Hence, the graph of (A) is not a function of x.

22. **(B)**

$$\frac{25\left(\frac{a}{b}\right)^3\left(\frac{c}{a}\right)^4}{125\left(\frac{a}{c}\right)^7\left(\frac{b}{c}\right)^{-2}} = \frac{\left(\frac{a}{b}\right)^3\left(\frac{c}{a}\right)^4}{5\left(\frac{a}{c}\right)^7\left(\frac{b}{c}\right)^{-2}}$$

$$= \frac{\dfrac{a^3}{b^3} \dfrac{c^4}{a^4}}{5\left(\dfrac{a^7}{c^7}\right)\left(\dfrac{b}{c}\right)^{-2}}$$

$$= \frac{\dfrac{c^4}{ab^3}}{5\left(\dfrac{a^7}{c^7}\right)\left(\dfrac{c}{b}\right)^{2}}$$

$$= \frac{\dfrac{c^4}{ab^3}}{5\dfrac{a^7}{c^7} \times \dfrac{c^2}{b^2}}$$

$$= \frac{\dfrac{c^4}{ab^3}}{5\dfrac{a^7}{b^2c^5}}$$

$$= \frac{c^4}{ab^3} \times \frac{b^2c^5}{5a^7}$$

$$= \frac{c^4}{ab} \times \frac{c^5}{5a^7}$$

$$= \frac{c^9}{5a^8b}$$

23.   **(B)**

$6(-4)^3 - 29(-4) + 35 = -384 + 116 + 35 = -233$

Calculator:

6 $\boxed{\times}$ 4 $\boxed{+/-}$ $\boxed{y^x}$ 3 $\boxed{-}$ 29 $\boxed{\times}$ 4 $\boxed{+/-}$ $\boxed{+}$ 35 $\boxed{=}$ -233

24.   **(B)**

Area of shaded region = area of parabola − area of triangle

$A = 36$ sq. units $- \left(\dfrac{1}{2}\right)(6)(9)$

$A = 36 - 27$

A = 9 sq. units

Calculator:

$$36 \; \boxed{-} \; 0.5 \; \boxed{\times} \; 6 \; \boxed{\times} \; 9 \; \boxed{=} \; 9$$

25.   **(E)**

$x1 =$ quiz avg., $x2 =$ test avg., and $x3 =$ final

$$x_w = \frac{w1(x1) + w2(x2) + w3(x3)}{100}$$

$$x_w = \frac{30(74.75) + 40(86.6667) + 30(83)}{100}$$

Calculator:

$$30 \; \boxed{\times} \; 74.75 \; \boxed{+} \; 40 \; \boxed{\times} \; 86.6667 \boxed{+} \; 30 \; \boxed{\times} \; 83 \; \boxed{=} \; \boxed{\div} \; 100 \; \boxed{=} \; 81.99$$

$x_w = 82\%$

26.   **(C)**

$$m = \frac{(\Delta y)}{(\Delta x)}$$

$$= \frac{(6-0)}{(4-0)}$$

$$= \frac{3}{2}$$

27.   **(E)**

$$\text{Area} = \left(\frac{1}{2}\right)bh + bh + \frac{1}{4}\pi r^2$$

$$= \left(\frac{1}{2}\right)(4)(6) + (2)(4) + \left(\frac{1}{4}\right)\pi 2^2$$

$$= 12 + 8 + 3.14$$

$$= 23.14$$

Calculator:

$$.5 \; \boxed{\times} \; 4 \; \boxed{\times} \; 6 \; \boxed{+} \; 2 \; \boxed{\times} \; 4 \; \boxed{+} \; .25 \; \boxed{\times} \; \boxed{\pi} \; \boxed{\times} \; 2 \; \boxed{x^2} \; \boxed{=} \; 23.14$$

28.   **(D)**

The ratio of their volumes is the cube of the ratio of their diameters.

Since the mass of a sphere is directly proportional to the volume, the ratio of their masses is equal to the ratio of their volumes.

$$\therefore \frac{\text{Mass of the bigger sphere}}{\text{Mass of the smaller sphere}} = \left(\frac{2}{1}\right)^3$$

Mass of the bigger sphere $= 120 \times 2^3$

$$= 120 \times 8$$

$$= 960$$

29.   **(E)**

$$f(-5) = \frac{-5}{5} - 3 = -4 \ .$$

$$f(15) = \frac{15}{5} - 3 = 0 \ .$$

Therefore, the range of $f(x)$ is $-4 < f(x) < 0$.

30.   **(C)**

From the trigonometric identity : $\sin^2\theta + \cos^2\theta = 1$

$$\sin\theta = \sqrt{1 - \cos^2\theta}$$

$$= \sqrt{1 - \left(\frac{x}{y}\right)^2}$$

$$= \sqrt{\frac{y^2 - x^2}{y^2}}$$

$$= \frac{\sqrt{y^2 - x^2}}{y}$$

$$\tan\theta = \frac{\sin\theta}{\cos\theta}$$

$$= \frac{\sqrt{y^2 - \frac{x^2}{y}}}{\frac{x}{y}}$$

$$= \frac{\sqrt{y^2 - x^2}}{x}$$

31.　　**(C)**

Probability of getting no heads $\quad = \left(\dfrac{1}{2}\right)^3$

$$= \frac{1}{8}$$

Probability of getting one head $\quad = 3 \times \left(\dfrac{1}{2}\right)^3$

$$= \frac{3}{8}$$

Since the events of getting no heads and one head are mutually exclusive, the probability of their union is the sum of their probabilities. Therefore,

Probability of getting at most one head $\quad = \dfrac{1}{8} + \dfrac{3}{8}$

$$= \frac{1}{2}$$

32.　　**(E)**

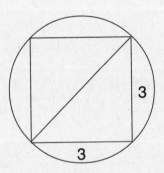

diameter $= \sqrt{3^2 + 3^2}$

$$= \sqrt{18}$$

$$= 3\sqrt{2}$$

$$\text{circumference} = 2 \times \pi \times \frac{3\sqrt{2}}{2}$$

$$= 3\pi\sqrt{2}$$

33.   **(B)**

The general equation of a parabola symmetrical about the y-axis is $y = ax^2 + c$. (Note: It only contains terms with an even power of x.)

Substitute the point $(0,-2)$ into the equation:

$$-2 = a(0)^2 + c$$

$$c = -2$$

Substitute $(2,0)$ and $c = -2$ into the equation:

$$0 = a(2)^2 + (-2)$$

$$0 = 4a - 2$$

$$a = \frac{1}{2}$$

Therefore, the equation of the parabola is $y = \frac{1}{2}x^2 - 2$.

34.   **(E)**

$$\text{Area of shaded region} = \frac{60°}{360°}\pi\, OB^2 - \frac{60°}{360°}\pi\, OA^2$$

$$= \frac{\pi}{6}\left((7+2)^2 - 7\right)$$

$$= \frac{\pi}{6}(81 - 49) = \frac{16\pi}{3}$$

35.   **(E)**

$$x^2 - 3x - 4 < 0$$

$$(x + 1)(x - 4) < 0$$

$$-1 < x < 4$$

36.   **(B)**

$$\text{Cost of an apple} = \frac{\$3.25}{5}$$

$$= \$0.65$$

Cost of an orange = $1.05 - $0.65

$$= \$0.40$$

37.　**(D)**

$\angle CDA = \angle CAD = 15°$　　　　　　$(\because AC = CD)$

$\angle CDB = \angle CBD = 15°$　　　　　　$(\because BC = CD)$

$\angle ADB = \angle CDA + \angle CDB$

$$= 15° + 15°$$

$$= 30°$$

Let $\angle CAB = \beta$

$\angle CBA = \angle CAB = \beta$　　　　$(\because AC = BC)$

$\angle ADB = (\beta + 15°) + (\beta + 15°) = 180°$

$(\because$ sum of interior $\angle$s of $\triangle ADB)$

$$30° + 2\beta + 30° = 180°$$

$$2\beta = 120°$$

$$\beta = 60°$$

$\theta + \beta + \beta = 180°$ $(\because$ sum of interior $\angle$s of $\triangle ACB)$

$\theta = 180° - 120°$

$\theta = 60°$

38.　**(C)**

If $(5 - x)$ and $(11 - x)$ are non-zero and have opposite signs, then $(5 - x)$ $(11 - x) < 0$, so x must lie between 5 and 11.

$$5 < x < 11$$

Thus, the least positive integer x from the solution set is 6.

39.　**(D)**

$n_1(\sin(30°)) = n_2(\sin(x))$

$1.000293(0.5) = 1.517(\sin(x))$

Calculator:

1.000293 $\boxed{\times}$ .5 $\boxed{\div}$ 1.517 $\boxed{=}$ 0.32969

$0.32969 = \sin(x)$

Using a second function key and then $\boxed{\sin}$ you will find that $0.32969 = 19.25°$.

$x \approx 19.25°$

40.   **(C)**

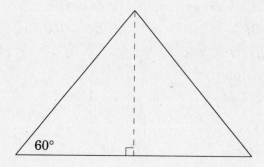

If the perimeter of an equilateral triangle is $7\frac{1}{2}$, each side is $\dfrac{\left(7\frac{1}{2}\right)}{3}$ or $2\frac{1}{2}$ units long, and each angle is $\dfrac{180°}{3}$ or $60°$.

$$h = 2\frac{1}{2}\sin 60°$$

$$= \frac{5}{2}\frac{\sqrt{3}}{2}$$

$$= \frac{5\sqrt{3}}{4}$$

$$\text{Area} = \frac{1}{2} \times \left(\frac{5}{2}\right)h$$

$$= \left(\frac{1}{2}\right)\left(\frac{5}{2}\right)\left(\frac{5\sqrt{3}}{4}\right)$$

$$= \frac{25\sqrt{3}}{16}$$

41.   **(D)**

$y = 2x + 1 \rightarrow y\text{-intercept} = (0, 1)$, so we may eliminate (A) and (C).

We may also eliminate (E) since the slope of y is 2, which is positive. Graph (B) indicates that the point (3, 2) is on the graph but if we substitute these values into the given equation we find the statement false. The only possibility therefore is graph (D).

42.　　**(E)**

I.　From trigonometric identity:

$$\tan\theta = \frac{\sin\theta}{\cos\theta}$$

II.　$\cos\phi = \sin(90° - \phi) = \sin\theta$

Similarly, $\sin\phi = \cos(90° - \phi) = \cos\theta$

Thus, $\dfrac{\cos\phi}{\sin\phi} = \dfrac{\sin\theta}{\cos\theta} = \tan\theta$

III.　$\tan\theta = \dfrac{\text{opposite side}}{\text{adjacent side}} = \dfrac{a}{b}$

Therefore, all of the above expressions are equal to $\tan\theta$.

43.　　**(E)**

Since the square of a real number is non-negative, $x^2 < -1$ and $x^2 < -4$ do not have solution sets on the real axis.

Consider a quadratic inequality of the form $ax^2 + bx + c > 0$.

If the discriminant $b^2 - 4ac$ is greater than or equal to zero, the inequality will have real roots; otherwise the roots are complex.

Note　　　$2^2 - (1)(2) = -4$

and　　　$1^2 - 4(-3)(-1) = -11.$

Therefore, none of the choices are correct.

44.　　**(C)**

$$\begin{cases} 3x + 2y = 5 & (1) \\ x - 4y = 1 & (2) \end{cases}$$

$$\begin{array}{rl} 2\ (1) & 6x + 4y = 10 \\ +\ (2) + & x - 4y = 1 \\ \hline & 7x = 11 \end{array}$$

$$x = \frac{11}{7}$$

Substitute $x = \dfrac{11}{7}$ into (2):

$$\frac{11}{7} - 4y = 1$$

$$4y = \frac{4}{7}$$

$$y = \frac{1}{7}$$

45. **(B)**

$c = 18a + 24b = 6(3a + 4b)$

Therefore, c is a multiple of 6 and must be divisible by 6.

46. **(C)**

This is a program which computes the summation of the first five integers starting from 1.

Therefore, SUM = $1 + 2 + 3 + 4 + 5 = 15$.

47. **(E)**

I. An odd integer times two will become an even integer. An even integer times any number will remain even. The sum of two even numbers is also an even number.

Therefore $2x + 3y$ must be even.

II. An even integer times any number will remain even. Therefore, xy must be even.

III. The sum of an odd integer and an even integer is odd. An odd integer minus one will become even. Therefore, $x + y - 1$ must be even.

48. **(C)**

$$\sin 2\theta = \frac{\sqrt{3}}{2}$$

$$2\theta = 60°$$

$$\theta = 30°$$

$(\cos\theta + \sin\theta)^2$

$= \cos^2\theta + 2\sin\theta\,\cos\theta + \sin^2\theta$

$= 1 + 2\cos\theta\,\sin\theta$

$= 1 + 2\cos 30°\sin 30°$

$$= 1 + 2\left(\frac{\sqrt{3}}{2}\right)\left(\frac{1}{2}\right)$$

$$= 1 + \frac{\sqrt{3}}{2}$$

49. **(A)**

   area I $= 5^2 - \pi (2.5)^2$

   Calculator:

   5 $\boxed{x^2}$ $\boxed{-}$ $\boxed{\pi}$ $\boxed{\times}$ 2.5 $\boxed{x^2}$ $\boxed{=}$ 5.365 sq. units

   area II $= (\pi)(3.535)^2 - 5^2 = 14.258$

   Calculator:

   $\boxed{\pi}$ $\boxed{\times}$ 3.535 $\boxed{x^2}$ $\boxed{-}$ 5 $\boxed{x^2}$ $\boxed{=}$ 14.258 sq. units

   14.258 $\boxed{-}$ 5.365 $\boxed{=}$ 8.893

   area II by 8.893 sq. units.

50. **(B)**

   $$\bar{x} = \frac{(2.5 + 4 + 3.5 + 1.5 + 5 + 4.5)}{6}$$

   Calculator:

   2.5 $\boxed{+}$ 4 $\boxed{+}$ 3.5 $\boxed{+}$ 1.5 $\boxed{+}$ 5 $\boxed{+}$ 4.5 $\boxed{=}$ $\boxed{\div}$ 6 $\boxed{=}$ 3.5

   $\bar{x} = 3.5$ million

THE SAT SUBJECT TEST IN

Math
Level 1

PRACTICE TEST 6

SAT Mathematics Level 1

Practice Test 6

Time: 1 Hour
50 Questions

DIRECTIONS: Choose the best answer for each question and mark the letter of your selection on the corresponding answer sheet.

NOTES:

(1) Some questions require the use of a calculator. You must decide when the use of your calculator will be helpful.

(2) Make sure your calculator is in degree mode.

(3) All figures are drawn to scale and lie in a plane unless otherwise stated.

(4) The domain of any function f is the set of all real numbers x for which $f(x)$ is a real number, unless other information is provided.

REFERENCE INFORMATION: The following information may be helpful in answering some of the questions.

Volume of a right circular cone with radius r and height h
$$V = \frac{1}{3}\pi r^2 h$$

Lateral area of a right circular cone with circumference c and slant height l
$$S = \frac{1}{2}cl$$

Volume of a sphere with radius r
$$V = \frac{4}{3}\pi r^3$$

Surface area of a sphere with radius r
$$S = 4\pi r^2$$

Volume of a pyramid with base area B and height h
$$V = \frac{1}{3}Bh$$

1. Given the equation $\dfrac{9x}{4} = (a^5 + 1)^5$; if $x = 3$, then a equals

(A) 0.675 .

(D) 1.832 .

(B) 0.858 .

(E) 0.5 .

(C) 0.425 .

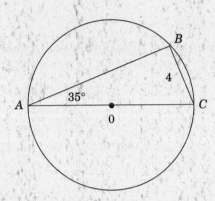

2.

In the figure, $\angle BAC = 35°$, $BC = 4$. Find the radius of the circle.

(A) 4.773

(D) 5.675

(B) 2.982

(E) 7.228

(C) 3.487

3. Car A and B are travelling 30 and 40 miles per hour, respectively. If car B starts out five miles behind car A, how many hours will it take for car B to overtake car A?

(A) $\dfrac{1}{2}$

(D) $\dfrac{3}{2}$

(B) $\dfrac{3}{4}$

(E) 2

(C) 1

4.

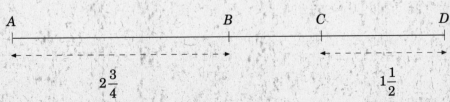

In the figure on previous page, if B is the midpoint of segment AD, then the length of segment AC is

(A) $3\dfrac{1}{2}$.

(D) $4\dfrac{1}{4}$.

(B) $3\dfrac{3}{4}$.

(E) 5.

(C) 4.

5. What are the coordinates of the midpoint between the points $(-2, 3)$ and $(4, -5)$?

(A) $(2, -1)$

(D) $(1, 1)$

(B) $(1, -1)$

(E) $(1, 2)$

(C) $(0, -1)$

6. If $\log_2(x + 5) = 4$, then $x =$

(A) -3.

(D) 9.

(B) 16.

(E) 11.

(C) 8.

7. If $\dfrac{2}{3}a = 2$, then $a - \dfrac{2}{3} =$

(A) $-\dfrac{1}{3}$.

(D) $\dfrac{7}{3}$.

(B) 0.

(E) 3.

(C) $\dfrac{1}{3}$.

8. If $-9 < x < -4$ and $-12 < y < -6$, then

(A) $0 < xy < 12$.

(D) $10 < xy < 24$.

(B) $108 < xy < 112$.

(E) $4 < xy < 12$.

(C) $24 < xy < 108$.

9.

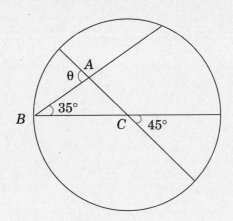

In the figure above, three chords of the circle intersect making the angles shown. What is the value of θ?

(A) 35°

(B) 45°

(C) 60°

(D) 75°

(E) 80°

10. If $\dfrac{a}{b} = \dfrac{2}{3}$, then $9a^2 - 4b^2 =$

(A) −6.

(B) −4.

(C) 0.

(D) 4.

(E) 6.

11. $3^{\sqrt{5x}} = 12$. Find x.

(A) 2.25

(B) 5.125

(C) 1.023

(D) 9.72

(E) 4.18

12. If $\dfrac{2}{\frac{x}{3}} = \dfrac{3}{7}$, then $x =$

(A) 6.

(B) 7.

(C) 9.

(D) 14.

(E) 16.

13. $\sqrt{108} + 3\sqrt{12} - 7\sqrt{3} =$

    (A) $3 - 3\sqrt{3}$ (D) $5\sqrt{3}$

    (B) 0   (E) $10\sqrt{3}$

    (C) $4\sqrt{3}$

14.

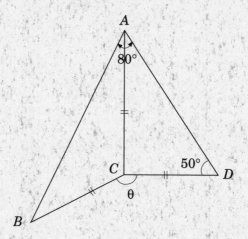

    In the figure above, if $AC = CB = CD$, then $\theta =$

    (A) 40°.   (D) 200°.

    (B) 120°.   (E) 220°.

    (C) 160°.

15. If $y = \dfrac{\dfrac{x^2+1}{2x^4+x^3+2}}{\dfrac{x}{4x^3+5}}$, and $x = 2$, then y equals

    (A) 0.3332 .   (D) 2.2024 .

    (B) 8.6728 .   (E) 1.8521 .

    (C) 3.7325 .

16. If an operation * is defined for all real numbers a and b by the relation $a * b = 2a + 3b$, then $3 * (-1) =$

   (A) −1.   (D) 2.

   (B) 0.   (E) 3.

   (C) 1.

17. In how many ways can we arrange four letters (a, b, c, and d) in different orders?

   (A) 4   (D) 24

   (B) 8   (E) 48

   (C) 16

18. If $x = 2^{3m} \times 3^{7m} \times 5^{\frac{m}{2}}$ and $m = 0.2$, then x equals

   (A) 8.29.   (D) 7.46.

   (B) 4.24.   (E) 5.32.

   (C) 1.27.

19. Six dice are thrown. What is the probability of getting six ones?

   (A) 0.0000214   (D) 0.1667

   (B) 0.0278   (E) 0.1

   (C) 0.00001

20.

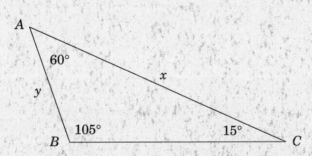

In the above figure, side y is 10 less than x. The length of x is

   (A) 13.66.   (D) 17.38.

   (B) 8.72.   (E) 16.27.

   (C) 3.65.

21. A rectangular solid has sides 5, 7, and 9. Find the volume of the largest sphere that can fit inside the rectangular solid.

(A) 32.70

(D) 14.37

(B) 65.45

(E) 49.22

(C) 40.08

22. If $abc \neq 0$, then $\dfrac{3a^2bc^3 + 9a^3b^2c}{27ab^2c + 15a^2b^2c^3} =$

(A) $\dfrac{ab(c^2 + 3)}{c(9 + 5a)}$.

(D) $\dfrac{c^2 + 3ab}{9 + 5ac^2}$.

(B) $\dfrac{a(c^2 + 3ab)}{b(9 + 5ac^2)}$.

(E) $\dfrac{a}{b(9 + 5ac^2)}$.

(C) $\dfrac{a(c^2 + 3ab)}{c(9 + ac^2)}$.

23. If $x = 1$ and $y = -2$, then $3x^2y - 2xy^2 + 5xy =$

(A) −36.

(D) 6.

(B) −24.

(E) 12.

(C) −1.

24. If $\log_{10}(x + 3) - \log_{10}(x - 1) = 1$, then $x =$

(A) 0.

(D) $\dfrac{16}{9}$.

(B) $\dfrac{11}{9}$.

(E) 2.

(C) $\dfrac{13}{9}$.

25. How many integers are in the solution set $|3x - 7| < 2$?

(A) None

(D) Three

(B) One

(E) Six

(C) Two

26.

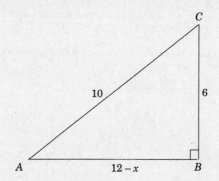

In right triangle ABC on the figure above, if $AC = 10$, $AB = 12 - x$, and $BC = 6$, then $x =$

(A) 0.

(B) 1.

(C) 2.

(D) 4.

(E) 6.

27. Which of the following is not the graph of a function of x?

(A)

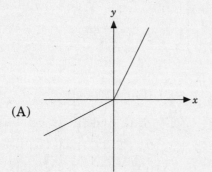

(B)

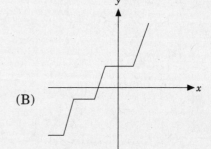

(C)

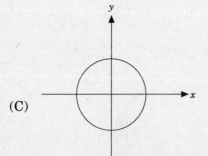

(D)

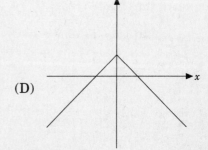

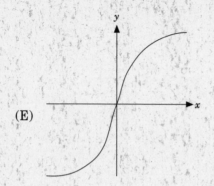

(E)

28. The distance between point (3, –7) and point (–4, 8) is

(A) 14.37 .

(D) 78.46 .

(B) 8.23 .

(E) 16.55 .

(C) 9.92 .

29. If x and y are positive integers, which of the following must be a positive integer?

I. $x + y$

II. $x - y$

III. $x\,y$

(A) I only

(D) I and III only

(B) II only

(E) I, II, and III

(C) I and II only

30. What is the equation of the line which has a slope equal to 2 and passes through the point (–1, 1)?

(A) $2x - y + 3 = 0$

(D) $x - 2y + 1 = 0$

(B) $2x - y + 1 = 0$

(E) $x - y + 3 = 0$

(C) $x - 2y + 3 = 0$

31.

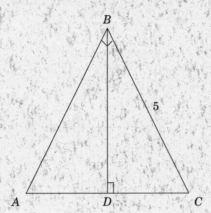

In the figure above, $BC = 5$, and the area of $\triangle ABC$ is 9.375. The area of $\triangle ABD$ is

(A) 3.375 .

(D) 3.965 .

(B) 4.287 .

(E) 5.728 .

(C) 2.976 .

32. If $0° \leq \theta \leq 90°$ and $\tan \theta = \sqrt{2}$, then the value of $\sin^2\theta(\tan^2\theta +1)$ is

(A) $\dfrac{\sqrt{2}}{2}$.

(D) 2 .

(B) 0 .

(E) $2\sqrt{2}$.

(C) 1 .

33. If $f(x) = 3x - 1$ and $g(f(x)) = x$, then $g(x) =$

(A) x

(D) $3x + 1$

(B) $\dfrac{x+1}{3}$

(E) $3x + 2$

(C) $\dfrac{x-1}{3}$

34.

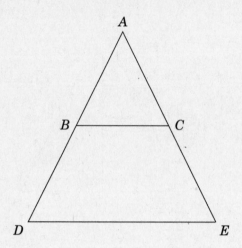

In the figure above, if $BC \parallel DE$ and if $AE = a$ and $AC = b$, then $\dfrac{BC}{DE} =$

(A) $\dfrac{b}{a}$.

(D) $a - b$.

(B) $1 - \dfrac{b}{a}$.

(E) None of the above.

(C) $1 + \dfrac{b}{a}$.

35. If $i^2 = -1$ and $y = 1 + 3i$, then $\dfrac{1}{y} =$

(A) $\dfrac{1}{10} - \dfrac{3}{10}i$.

(D) $1 - 3i$.

(B) $\dfrac{1}{4} - \dfrac{3}{4}i$.

(E) $1 + 9i$.

(C) $-\dfrac{1}{2} + \dfrac{3}{2}i$.

36.

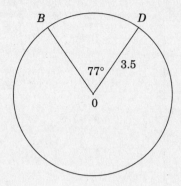

In the above figure, the area *BOD* is

(A) 5.77 .   (D) 8.23 .

(B) 4.25 .   (E) 7.65 .

(C) 13.44 .

37. Find the area enclosed by the line $y = -3.25x + 7.85$, the x-axis, and the y-axis.

(A) 8.62   (D) 5.44

(B) 9.48   (E) 11.25

(C) 6.37

38. If $\dfrac{1}{a} = \dfrac{1}{\frac{1}{b}}$ and $2 < a < 5$, then

(A) $\dfrac{1}{2} > b > \dfrac{1}{5}$.   (D) $\dfrac{-1}{5} > b > \dfrac{-1}{2}$.

(B) $2 > b > \dfrac{1}{2}$.   (E) $\dfrac{-1}{2} > b > -2$.

(C) $5 > b > 2$.

39.

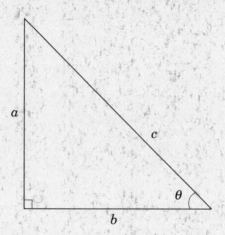

In the right triangle in the figure above, $\tan\theta$ is equal to which of the following?

I. $\dfrac{a}{b}$

II. $\dfrac{\sin\theta}{\cos\theta}$

III. $\dfrac{a}{\sqrt{a^2+b^2}}$

(A) I only.

(B) II only.

(C) III only.

(D) I and II only.

(E) I and III only.

40. If $0° < \theta < 90°$ and $\sin\theta = \dfrac{a}{b}$, then $\tan\theta =$

(A) $\dfrac{a}{\sqrt{a^2-b^2}}$.

(B) $\dfrac{a}{\sqrt{b^2-a^2}}$.

(C) $\dfrac{a}{a^2+b^2}$.

(D) $\dfrac{b}{\sqrt{a^2-b^2}}$.

(E) $\dfrac{b}{\sqrt{b^2-a^2}}$.

41. If $x \neq 0$, then $(125^{2x})(5^x) =$

(A) 5^{3x}.

(D) 5^{7x}.

(B) 5^{4x}.

(E) 5^{9x}.

(C) 5^{5x}.

42. The coordinates of the point of intersection of the lines having equations $\sqrt{3}\,x + 3y = 2$ and $x - \sqrt{3}\,y = \sqrt{3}$ are

(A) $\left(\dfrac{5}{2\sqrt{3}}, -\dfrac{1}{6} \right)$.

(D) $\left(-\dfrac{1}{\sqrt{3}}, \dfrac{1}{2\sqrt{3}} \right)$.

(B) $\left(\dfrac{1}{2\sqrt{3}}, -\dfrac{1}{\sqrt{3}} \right)$.

(E) $\left(-\dfrac{1}{2\sqrt{3}}, \dfrac{5}{2\sqrt{3}} \right)$.

(C) $\left(-\dfrac{1}{\sqrt{3}}, \dfrac{1}{\sqrt{3}} \right)$.

43. If $\dfrac{5}{x-2} + \dfrac{2}{2x+1} = \dfrac{1}{x}$, then $x =$

(A) $\dfrac{-1 \pm 2}{5}$.

(D) $-2 \pm 3\sqrt{-1}$.

(B) $\dfrac{-2 \pm 2}{5}$.

(E) $\dfrac{-1 \pm 2\sqrt{-1}}{5}$.

(C) $-1 \pm 2\sqrt{-1}$.

44. Given a line $y = 4x + 9$ and a point $(10, 4)$, the distance of the point to the line is

(A) 10.9.

(D) 2.6.

(B) 12.3.

(E) 3.8.

(C) 4.7.

45. Calculate $\dfrac{\sin 40^\circ \cos^2 37^\circ}{\tan 82^\circ \sin 21^\circ}$.

(A) 1.257

(D) 0.161

(B) 6.283

(E) 0.052

(C) 3.107

46. Which of the following represents the graph of the equation $x = |y - 2|$?

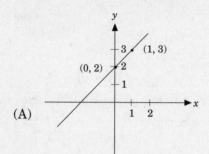

(A)

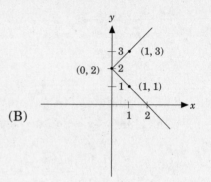

(B)

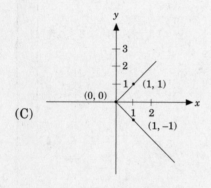

(C)

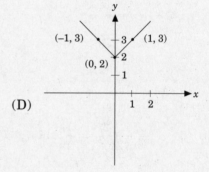

(D)

(E) None of the above

47. If $\log_8 x = \dfrac{4}{3}$, then $x =$

(A) 1.

(D) 8.

(B) 2.

(E) 16.

(C) 4.

48. If the sum of three consecutive odd numbers is 51, then the first odd number of the sequence is

(A) 11.

(D) 17.

(B) 13.

(E) 19.

(C) 15.

49. If $x = \sqrt{3}$ and $y = \sqrt{2}$, then $(2x + 3y)(x + y) =$

(A) $6 + \sqrt{6}$.

(D) $10 + 5\sqrt{6}$.

(B) $6 + 3\sqrt{6}$.

(E) $12 + 5\sqrt{6}$.

(C) $9 + 2\sqrt{6}$.

50. If $xy \neq 0$, then $\dfrac{\dfrac{1}{x} - \dfrac{1}{y}}{\dfrac{1}{x^2} - \dfrac{1}{y^2}} =$

(A) $\dfrac{xy}{x + y}$.

(D) $\dfrac{-xy}{x - y}$.

(B) xy.

(E) $\dfrac{xy}{x - y}$.

(C) $\dfrac{1}{x + y}$.

TEST 6

ANSWER KEY

1. (B)	14. (C)	27. (C)	40. (B)
2. (C)	15. (D)	28. (E)	41. (D)
3. (A)	16. (E)	29. (D)	42. (A)
4. (C)	17. (D)	30. (A)	43. (E)
5. (B)	18. (A)	31. (A)	44. (A)
6. (E)	19. (A)	32. (D)	45. (D)
7. (D)	20. (A)	33. (B)	46. (B)
8. (C)	21. (B)	34. (A)	47. (E)
9. (E)	22. (B)	35. (A)	48. (C)
10. (C)	23. (B)	36. (D)	49. (E)
11. (C)	24. (C)	37. (B)	50. (A)
12. (D)	25. (B)	38. (A)	
13. (D)	26. (D)	39. (D)	

DETAILED EXPLANATIONS
OF ANSWERS

1. **(B)**

Rearrange the equation so that a is singled out to be at one side of the equation, i.e.,

$$5\sqrt{\frac{9x}{4}} = a^5 + 1$$

$$5\sqrt{\frac{9x}{4}} - 1 = a^5$$

$$5\sqrt{5\sqrt{\frac{9x}{4}} - 1} = a$$

Because $x = 3$,

$$a = 5\sqrt{5\sqrt{\frac{9^x 3}{4}} - 1}$$

Calculator:

9 $\boxed{\times}$ 3 $\boxed{\div}$ 4 $\boxed{=}$ $\boxed{y^x}$ 0.2 $\boxed{=}$ -1 $\boxed{=}$ $\boxed{y^x}$ 0.2 $\boxed{=}$ 0.858

2. **(C)**

First of all, notice $\angle ABC = 90°$ and $AC = 28$. So, $\triangle ABC$ is a right triangle.

Then,

$$\frac{BC}{AC} = \sin \angle BAC$$

or

$$\frac{4}{28} = \sin 35°$$

or

$$r = \frac{4}{2}\frac{1}{\sin 35°}$$

By using your calculator, you can easily find that $r = 3.487$.

Calculator:

2 $\boxed{\div}$ 35 $\boxed{\sin}$ $\boxed{=}$ 3.487

3.　　**(A)**

Let x be the number of hours car B takes to overtake car A.

$$30x + 5 = 40x$$
$$10x = 5$$
$$x = \frac{1}{2} \ .$$

4.　　**(C)**

$$
\begin{aligned}
AC &= AD - CD \\
&= 2AB - CD \quad \text{(as } AD = 2AB\text{)} \\
&= 2 \times 2\frac{3}{4} - 1\frac{1}{2} \\
&= \frac{22}{4} - \frac{6}{4} \\
&= \frac{16}{4} \\
&= 4
\end{aligned}
$$

5.　　**(B)**

$$x = \frac{x_1 + x_2}{2}$$
$$= \frac{-2 + 4}{2}$$
$$= 1$$

$$y = \frac{y_1 + y_2}{2}$$
$$= \frac{3 + (-5)}{2}$$
$$= -1$$

The coordinates of the midpoint are $(x, y) = (1, -1)$.

6.　　**(E)**

$$\log_2(x + 5) = 4$$
$$x + 5 = 244$$

$$x + 5 = 16$$
$$x = 11$$

7.   **(D)**

$$\frac{2}{3}a = 2$$

$$a = 3$$

$$a - \frac{2}{3} = 3 - \frac{2}{3} = \frac{7}{3}$$

8.   **(C)**

$$(-4)(-6) < xy < (-9)(-12)$$
$$24 < xy < 108$$

9.   **(E)**

$\angle ACB = 45°$ (vertically opposite angles)

$$\theta = \angle ABC + \angle ACB$$
$$= 35° + 45°$$
$$= 80°$$

10.   **(C)**

$$\frac{a}{b} = \frac{2}{3}$$

$$a = \frac{2b}{3}$$

Substitute $a = \dfrac{2b}{3}$ into the given expression:

$$9a^2 - 4b^2 = 9\left(\frac{2}{3}b\right)^2 - 4b^2$$

$$= 9\left(\frac{4}{9}b^2\right) - 4b^2$$

$$= 4b^2 - 4b^2 = 0$$

11.   **(C)**

  Take log on both sides of the equation,

$$\log 3^{\sqrt{5x}} = \log 12$$

or

So, $$x = \frac{1}{5}\left(\frac{\log 12}{\log 3}\right)^2$$

Calculator:

  12 $\boxed{\log}$ $\boxed{\div}$ 3 $\boxed{\log}$ $\boxed{=}$ $\boxed{x^2}$ $\boxed{\div}$ 5 $\boxed{=}$ 1.023

12.   **(D)**

$$\frac{2}{\dfrac{x}{3}} = \frac{3}{7}$$

  $14 = x$ (cross multiply)

13.   **(D)**

$$\sqrt{108} + 3\sqrt{12} - 7\sqrt{3} = \sqrt{(36)(3)} + 3\sqrt{(4)(3)} - 7\sqrt{3}$$

$$= 6\sqrt{3} + 3\left(2\sqrt{3}\right) - 7\sqrt{3}$$

$$= 6\sqrt{3} + 6\sqrt{3} - 7\sqrt{3}$$

$$= 5\sqrt{3}$$

14.   **(C)**

$\angle CAD$ = $\angle CDA = 50°$ (as $\triangle ACD$ is isosceles)

$\angle ACD$ = $180° - 2 \times 50°$ (sum of interior angles of a $\triangle$)

    = $80°$

$\angle CAB$ = $80° - \angle CAD$

    = $80° - 50°$

    = $30°$

$\angle CAB$ = $\angle CBA = 30°$ (as $\triangle ACB$ is isosceles)

$$\angle ACB \;=\; 180° - 2 \times 30° \quad \text{(sum of interior angles of a } \Delta\text{)}$$

$$= \; 120°$$

$$\theta + \angle ACD + \angle ACB = 360°$$

$$\theta + 80° + 120° = 360°$$

$$\theta \;=\; 160°$$

15.   **(D)**

Replacing x by 2 in the equation:

$$y = \frac{\dfrac{2^2+1}{2.2^4+8+2}{2}}{4 \times 2^3 + 5}$$

$$= \frac{\dfrac{5}{3^2+10}{2}}{3^2+5}$$

$$= \frac{\dfrac{5}{42}{2}}{27}$$

$$= \frac{5 \times 37}{2 \times 42}$$

Calculator:

$$5 \;\boxed{\times}\; 37 \;\boxed{\div}\; 2 \;\boxed{\times}\; 42 \;\boxed{=}\; 2.20238$$

16.   **(E)**

$$3 * (-1) = 2(3) + 3(-1)$$

$$= 3$$

17.   **(D)**

Choose a to be the first letter:

abcd, abdc, acbd, acdb, adbc, adcb

Since each letter can be the first letter, there will be $4 \times 6 = 24$ different arrangements. $n!$ is the number of ways we can arrange n different objects.

$$n! = n(n-1)(n-2)...(1) \therefore 4! = 4(3)(2)(1) = 24$$

18.   **(A)**

Replacing m by 0.2 in each of the items:

$$x = 2^{3\times0.2} \times 3^{7\times0.2} \times 5^{\frac{0.2}{2}}$$

Calculator:

$$x = 1.5157 \boxed{\times} 4.6555 \boxed{\times} 1.1746$$

$$= 8.288$$

19.   **(A)**

The six throws are independent events.

Thus,

$$P(6 \text{ ones}) = P(1) \times P(1) \times P(1) \times P(1) \times P(1) \times P(1)$$

$$= \frac{1}{6} \times \frac{1}{6} \times \frac{1}{6} \times \frac{1}{6} \times \frac{1}{6} \times \frac{1}{6}$$

$$= \frac{1}{6^6}$$

Calculator:

$$6 \boxed{y^x} \ 6 \boxed{=} \ \boxed{1/x} = 0.000021433$$

20.   **(A)**

Apply the laws of tangents to the sides x and y, angles B and C. Then, we have

$$\frac{x-y}{x+y} = \frac{\tan\frac{1}{2}(B-C)}{\tan\frac{1}{2}(B+C)}$$

But,

$$\frac{1}{2}(B-C) = \frac{1}{2}(105-15) = 45 \ ;$$

$$\frac{1}{2}(B+C) = \frac{1}{2}(105+15) = 60$$

So, the right side is

$$\frac{\tan\frac{1}{2}(B-C)}{\tan\frac{1}{2}(B+C)} = \frac{\tan 45}{\tan 60} = \frac{1}{\sqrt{3}} .$$

According to the question, the left side is

$$\frac{x-y}{x+y} = \frac{10}{x+y} = \frac{10}{2x-10}$$

The whole equation becomes

$$\frac{10}{2x-10} = \frac{1}{\sqrt{3}}$$

or $\qquad\qquad 2x = 10 + 10\sqrt{3}$

or $\qquad\qquad x = 5 + 5\sqrt{3}$

Calculator:

$5\ \boxed{+}\ 5\ \boxed{\times}\ 3\ \boxed{\sqrt{}}\ \boxed{=}\ 13.66$

21. **(B)**

The diameter of the largest sphere inside the rectangular solid is 5, the smallest side of the solid. So, the volume of the sphere is

$$V = \frac{4}{3}\pi r^3 = \frac{4}{3}\pi\left(\frac{5}{2}\right)^3$$

Calculator:

$4\ \boxed{\div}\ 3\ \boxed{\times}\ \boxed{\pi}\ \boxed{\times}\ 2.5\ \boxed{y^x}\ 3\ \boxed{=}\ 65.45$

22. **(B)**

$$\frac{3a^2bc^3 + 9a^3b^2c}{27ab^2c + 15a^2b^2c^3} = \frac{3a^2bc(c^2 + 3ab)}{3ab^2c(9 + 5ac^2)}$$

$$= \frac{a(c^2 + 3ab)}{b(9 + 5ac^2)}$$

23. **(B)**

$$3x^2y - 2xy^2 + 5xy \quad = \quad xy(3x - 2y + 5)$$
$$= \quad (1)(-2)[3(1) - 2(-2) + 5]$$

$$= -2[3 + 4 + 5]$$
$$= -24$$

24.   **(C)**

$$\log_{10}(x + 3) - \log_{10}(x - 1) = 1$$

$$\log_{10}\frac{x+3}{x-1} = \log_{10} 10$$

$$\frac{x+3}{x-1} = 10$$

$$x + 3 = 10x - 10$$

$$13 = 9x$$

$$x = \frac{13}{9}$$

25.   **(B)**

$|3x - 7| < 2$

$-2 < 3x - 7 < 2$

$5 < 3x < 9$

$\dfrac{5}{3} < x < 3$

Therefore, the solution set is {2} and contains only one element.

26.   **(D)**

$(12 - x)^2 + 6^2 = 10^2$ (Pythagorean theorem)

$(12 - x)^2 = 100 - 36$

$(12 - x)^2 = 64$

$x = 4$ or 20

We reject the value $x = 20$ because that would imply $AB = -8$ and AB cannot be negative.

27.   **(C)**

The definition of a function guarantees a unique value of one variable when the other variable is known. A simple test for this property is to draw any vertical line and see that the line intersects the graph in at most one point. The graph of the circle fails this test. The equation for the circle is

$$x^2 + y^2 = r^2$$

$$x^2 = r^2 - y^2$$

$$x = \pm\sqrt{r^2 - y^2}$$

$$y = \pm\sqrt{r^2 - x^2}$$

Observe that for each value of y, two values of x can be obtained. Likewise, for each value of x, two values of y can be obtained. Since the uniqueness is no longer true, the above equation is not a function.

28.   **(E)**

The distance between point (x_1, y_1) and point (x_2, y_2) is

$$D = \sqrt{(x_1 - x_2)^2 + (y_1 - y_2)^2}$$

Therefore, for the points given,

$$D = \sqrt{(3+4)^2 + (-7-8)^2}$$

$$= \sqrt{49 + (15)^2}$$

Calculator:

$\boxed{()}$ 49 $\boxed{+}$ 15 $\boxed{x^2}$ $\boxed{()}$ $\boxed{\sqrt{}}$ = 16.55

29.   **(D)**

I.   The sum of two positive integers is always a positive integer. Therefore, $x + y$ is a positive integer.

II.   If x is less than y, then $x - y$ is negative.

III. The product of two positive integers is always a positive integer.

30.   **(A)**

The equation of the line is obtained from the point-slope equation

$$\frac{y - 1}{x - (-1)} = 2$$

$$\frac{y - 1}{x + 1} = 2$$

$$y - 1 = 2x + 2$$

$$2x - y + 3 = 0$$

31.   **(A)**

First, notice the area of $\triangle ABC$ is

$$A = \frac{1}{2} AB \times BC.$$

Since $BC = 5$,

$$AB = 2 \times A \; \frac{1}{BC} = 2 \times 9.375 \times \frac{1}{5}$$

Calculator:

   $2 \;\boxed{\times}\; 9.375 \;\boxed{\div}\; 5 \;\boxed{=}\; 3.75$

Then, AC can easily be found,

$$AC = \sqrt{3.75^2 + 5^2}$$

Calculator:

   $3.75 \;\boxed{x^2}\; \boxed{+}\; 5 \;\boxed{x^2}\; \boxed{=}\; \boxed{\sqrt{}} = 6.25$

BD can easily be found because

$$\frac{BD}{BC} = \frac{AB}{AC}$$

or $$BD = BC \; \frac{AB}{AC} = 5 \frac{3.75}{6.25}$$

Calculator:

   $5 \;\boxed{\times}\; 3.75 \;\boxed{\div}\; 6.25 \;\boxed{=}\; 3$

Obviously, $DC = 4$ (because $BC^2 = BD^2 + DC^2$). The area of $\triangle BDC$ is

$$\frac{1}{2} BD \times DC = 6.$$

So, the area of $\triangle ABD$ is

$$9.375 - 6 = 3.375$$

32.   **(D)**

$$\sin^2\theta(\tan^2\theta+1)=\sin^2\theta\left(\frac{\sin^2\theta}{\cos^2\theta}+1\right)$$

$$=\sin^2\theta\left(\frac{\sin^2\theta+\cos^2\theta}{\cos^2\theta}\right)$$

$$=\sin^2\theta\left(\frac{1}{\cos^2\theta}\right)$$

$$=\tan^2\theta$$

$$=\left(\sqrt{2}\right)^2$$

$$=2$$

33.   **(B)**

Since $g(f(x)) = x$, $g(x)$ is the inverse function of $f(x)$.

Let $y = f(x) = 3x - 1$.

Interchange x and y to obtain the inverse of $f(x)$.

$$x = 3y - 1$$

$$3y = x + 1$$

$$y = \frac{x+1}{3}$$

34.   **(A)**

Since $BC||DE$, $\triangle ABC$ is similar to $\triangle ADE$. Therefore,

$$\frac{AB}{AD} = \frac{BC}{DE} = \frac{AC}{AE} = \frac{b}{a}$$

Thus, $\dfrac{BC}{DE} = \dfrac{b}{a}$

35. **(A)**

$$\frac{1}{y} = \frac{1}{1+3i} \times \frac{1-3i}{1-3i}$$

$$= \frac{1-3i}{1^2 - 3^2 i^2}$$

$$= \frac{1-3i}{10}$$

$$= \frac{1}{10} - \frac{3}{10}i$$

36. **(D)**

The total amount of angle within a circle is 360°. Therefore, an area of 77° angle is $\frac{77°}{360°}$ of the total area of the circle, i.e., πr^2.

So, the area of *BOD* is

$$\frac{77°}{360°}\pi r^2 = \frac{77}{360}\pi \times 3.5^2$$

Calculator:

77 ÷ 360° × π × 3.5 x^2 = 8.23

37. **(B)**

The line $y = -3.25x + 7.85$ is shown in the graph

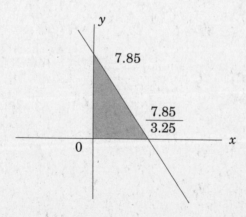

where the line intersects the x-axis at $\dfrac{7.85}{3.25}$ and the y-axis at 7.85; the shaded area is what we need to find. Obviously this area equals

$$\dfrac{7.85 \times \dfrac{7.85}{3.25}}{2}$$

Calculator:

$7.85\ \boxed{\times}\ 7.85\ \boxed{\div}\ 3.25\ \boxed{\div}\ 2\ \boxed{=}\ 9.48$

38.   **(A)**

$$\dfrac{1}{a} = \dfrac{1}{\dfrac{1}{b}}$$

$$a = \dfrac{1}{b}$$

Substitute $a = \dfrac{1}{b}$ into the given inequality:

$$2 < a < 5$$

$$2 < \dfrac{1}{b} < 5$$

$$\dfrac{1}{2} > b > \dfrac{1}{5}$$

39.   **(D)**

I. $\tan\theta = \dfrac{\text{opposite side}}{\text{adjacent side}} = \dfrac{a}{b}$

II. $\tan\theta = \dfrac{\sin\theta}{\cos\theta}$ (trigonometric identity)

III. $\tan\theta \neq \dfrac{a}{\sqrt{a^2 + b^2}}$

Therefore, (D) is the answer.

40.   **(B)**

From the trigonometric identity $\sin^2\theta + \cos^2\theta = 1$,

$$\sin^2\theta + \cos^2\theta = 1$$

$$\cos\theta = \sqrt{1 - \sin^2\theta}$$

$$\cos\theta = \sqrt{1 - \left(\frac{a}{b}\right)^2}$$

$$\cos\theta = \sqrt{\frac{b^2 - a^2}{b^2}}$$

$$\cos\theta = \frac{\sqrt{b^2 - a^2}}{b}$$

$$\tan\theta = \frac{\sin\theta}{\cos\theta}$$

$$= \left(\frac{a}{b}\right)\left(\frac{b}{\sqrt{b^2 - a^2}}\right)$$

$$= \frac{a}{\sqrt{b^2 - a^2}}$$

41.   **(D)**

$$\left(125^{2x}\right)\left(5^x\right) = \left(5^3\right)^{2x}\left(5^x\right)$$

$$= \left(5^{6x}\right)\left(5^x\right)$$

$$= 5^{6x+x} = 5^{7x}$$

42.   **(A)**

$$\begin{cases} \sqrt{3}x + 3y = 2 & (1) \\ x - \sqrt{3}y = \sqrt{3} & (2) \end{cases}$$

Multiply equation (2) by $\sqrt{3}$ and add equation (1).

$$\sqrt{3}x + 3y = 2$$
$$\underline{\sqrt{3}x - 3y = 2}$$
$$2\sqrt{3}x = 5$$
$$x = \frac{5}{2\sqrt{3}}$$

Substitute $x = \dfrac{5}{2\sqrt{3}}$ into (2):

$$\frac{5}{2\sqrt{3}} - \sqrt{3}y = \sqrt{3}$$

$$\sqrt{3}y = \frac{5}{2\sqrt{3}} - \sqrt{3}$$

$$y = \frac{5}{2(3)} - 1$$

$$y = \frac{5}{6} - 1$$

$$y = -\frac{1}{6}$$

Therefore, $\left(\dfrac{5}{2\sqrt{3}}, -\dfrac{1}{6}\right)$ are the coordinates of the point of intersection.

43.　　**(E)**

$$\frac{5}{x-2} + \frac{2}{2x+1} = \frac{1}{x}$$

$$\frac{5(2x+1) + 2(x-2)}{(x-2)(2x+1)} = \frac{1}{x}$$

$$\frac{10x + 5 + 2x - 4}{(x-2)(2x+1)} = \frac{1}{x}$$

$$\frac{12x + 1}{(x-2)(2x+1)} = \frac{1}{x}$$

$$x(12x + 1) = (x - 2)(2x + 1)$$

$$12x^2 + x = 2x^2 + x - 4x - 2$$

$$12x^2 + x = 2x^2 - 3x - 2$$

$$10x^2 + 4x + 2 = 0$$

$$5x^2 + 2x + 1 = 0$$

$$x = \frac{-2 \pm \sqrt{2^2 - 4(5)(1)}}{2(5)}$$

$$x = \frac{-2 \pm \sqrt{-16}}{2(5)}$$

$$x = \frac{-1 \pm \sqrt{-4}}{5}$$

$$x = \frac{-1 \pm 2\sqrt{-1}}{5}$$

44.   (A)

The relation that gives the distance between a point with coordinates (x_1, y_1) and a straight line of the form $ax + by = c$ is

$$d = \left| \frac{ax_1 + by_1 - c}{\sqrt{a^2 + b^2}} \right|$$

We are given both the point, $(x_1, y_1) = (10, 4)$, and the line, $y = 4x + 9$, but we must get this in the proper form $ax + by = c$. Subtracting $4x$ from both sides:

$$y - 4x = 9$$

or $$-4x + y = 9$$

in the equation $a = -4$, $b = 1$, and $c = 9$. Substituting these values back into the formula,

$$d = \left| \frac{(-4)(10) + (1)(4) - 9}{\sqrt{(-4)^2 + (1)^2}} \right|$$

$$= \left| \frac{-40 + 4 - 9}{\sqrt{16 + 1}} \right|$$

$$= \left| \frac{-45}{\sqrt{17}} \right|$$

Calculator:

45 $\boxed{\div}$ 17 $\boxed{\sqrt{}}$ $\boxed{=}$ 10.9

45. **(D)**

Calculator:

$$40 \; \boxed{\sin} = 0.6427$$

$$37 \; \boxed{\cos} \; \boxed{y^x} \; 2 = 0.6378$$

$$82 \; \boxed{\tan} = 7.11$$

$$21 \; \boxed{\sin} = 0.358$$

Then,

$$\frac{\sin 40° \cos^2 37°}{\tan 82° \sin 21°} = \frac{0.6427 \times 0.6378}{7.11 \times 0.358} = 0.161$$

By using your calculator, you can easily find that the answer is 0.161.

46. **(B)**

Substitute $x = 0$ into the given equation to obtain the y-intercept.

$$x = |y - 2|$$
$$0 = |y - 2|$$
$$y = 2$$

Therefore, the y-intercept of the equation is 2. Also, the graph of the given equation is symmetric about the line $y = 2$.

47. **(E)**

$$\log_8 x = \frac{4}{3}$$

$$x = (8)^{\frac{4}{3}}$$

$$x = \left[(8)^{\frac{1}{3}} \right]^4$$

$$x = [2]^4$$

$$x = 16$$

48. **(C)**

Let x be the first odd number. Then,

$$x + (x + 2) + (x + 4) = 51$$
$$3x + 6 = 51$$
$$3x = 45$$
$$x = 15$$

49. **(E)**

$$(2x + 3y)(x + y) = 2x^2 + 2xy + 3xy + 3y^2$$

$$= 2x^2 + 5xy + 3y^2$$

$$= 2(\sqrt{3})^2 + 5(\sqrt{3})(\sqrt{2}) + 3(\sqrt{2})^2$$

$$= 2(3) + 5\sqrt{6} + 3(2)$$

$$= 12 + 5\sqrt{6}$$

50. **(A)**

$$\frac{\dfrac{1}{x} - \dfrac{1}{y}}{\dfrac{1}{x^2} - \dfrac{1}{y^2}} = \left(\frac{1}{x} - \frac{1}{y}\right)\left(\frac{1}{x^2} - \frac{1}{y^2}\right)^{-1}$$

$$= \left(\frac{y - x}{xy}\right)\left(\frac{y^2 - x^2}{x^2 y^2}\right)^{-1}$$

$$= \left(\frac{y - x}{xy}\right)\left(\frac{x^2 y^2}{y^2 - x^2}\right)$$

$$= (x - y)\left(\frac{xy}{(x + y)(x - y)}\right)$$

$$= \frac{xy}{x + y}$$

THE SAT SUBJECT TEST IN

Math
Level 1

ANSWER SHEETS

SAT Math Level 1

Practice Test 1

1. Ⓐ Ⓑ Ⓒ Ⓓ Ⓔ
2. Ⓐ Ⓑ Ⓒ Ⓓ Ⓔ
3. Ⓐ Ⓑ Ⓒ Ⓓ Ⓔ
4. Ⓐ Ⓑ Ⓒ Ⓓ Ⓔ
5. Ⓐ Ⓑ Ⓒ Ⓓ Ⓔ
6. Ⓐ Ⓑ Ⓒ Ⓓ Ⓔ
7. Ⓐ Ⓑ Ⓒ Ⓓ Ⓔ
8. Ⓐ Ⓑ Ⓒ Ⓓ Ⓔ
9. Ⓐ Ⓑ Ⓒ Ⓓ Ⓔ
10. Ⓐ Ⓑ Ⓒ Ⓓ Ⓔ
11. Ⓐ Ⓑ Ⓒ Ⓓ Ⓔ
12. Ⓐ Ⓑ Ⓒ Ⓓ Ⓔ
13. Ⓐ Ⓑ Ⓒ Ⓓ Ⓔ
14. Ⓐ Ⓑ Ⓒ Ⓓ Ⓔ
15. Ⓐ Ⓑ Ⓒ Ⓓ Ⓔ
16. Ⓐ Ⓑ Ⓒ Ⓓ Ⓔ
17. Ⓐ Ⓑ Ⓒ Ⓓ Ⓔ
18. Ⓐ Ⓑ Ⓒ Ⓓ Ⓔ
19. Ⓐ Ⓑ Ⓒ Ⓓ Ⓔ
20. Ⓐ Ⓑ Ⓒ Ⓓ Ⓔ
21. Ⓐ Ⓑ Ⓒ Ⓓ Ⓔ
22. Ⓐ Ⓑ Ⓒ Ⓓ Ⓔ
23. Ⓐ Ⓑ Ⓒ Ⓓ Ⓔ
24. Ⓐ Ⓑ Ⓒ Ⓓ Ⓔ
25. Ⓐ Ⓑ Ⓒ Ⓓ Ⓔ

26. Ⓐ Ⓑ Ⓒ Ⓓ Ⓔ
27. Ⓐ Ⓑ Ⓒ Ⓓ Ⓔ
28. Ⓐ Ⓑ Ⓒ Ⓓ Ⓔ
29. Ⓐ Ⓑ Ⓒ Ⓓ Ⓔ
30. Ⓐ Ⓑ Ⓒ Ⓓ Ⓔ
31. Ⓐ Ⓑ Ⓒ Ⓓ Ⓔ
32. Ⓐ Ⓑ Ⓒ Ⓓ Ⓔ
33. Ⓐ Ⓑ Ⓒ Ⓓ Ⓔ
34. Ⓐ Ⓑ Ⓒ Ⓓ Ⓔ
35. Ⓐ Ⓑ Ⓒ Ⓓ Ⓔ
36. Ⓐ Ⓑ Ⓒ Ⓓ Ⓔ
37. Ⓐ Ⓑ Ⓒ Ⓓ Ⓔ
38. Ⓐ Ⓑ Ⓒ Ⓓ Ⓔ
39. Ⓐ Ⓑ Ⓒ Ⓓ Ⓔ
40. Ⓐ Ⓑ Ⓒ Ⓓ Ⓔ
41. Ⓐ Ⓑ Ⓒ Ⓓ Ⓔ
42. Ⓐ Ⓑ Ⓒ Ⓓ Ⓔ
43. Ⓐ Ⓑ Ⓒ Ⓓ Ⓔ
44. Ⓐ Ⓑ Ⓒ Ⓓ Ⓔ
45. Ⓐ Ⓑ Ⓒ Ⓓ Ⓔ
46. Ⓐ Ⓑ Ⓒ Ⓓ Ⓔ
47. Ⓐ Ⓑ Ⓒ Ⓓ Ⓔ
48. Ⓐ Ⓑ Ⓒ Ⓓ Ⓔ
49. Ⓐ Ⓑ Ⓒ Ⓓ Ⓔ
50. Ⓐ Ⓑ Ⓒ Ⓓ Ⓔ

SAT Math Level 1

Practice Test 2

1. Ⓐ Ⓑ Ⓒ Ⓓ Ⓔ   26. Ⓐ Ⓑ Ⓒ Ⓓ Ⓔ
2. Ⓐ Ⓑ Ⓒ Ⓓ Ⓔ   27. Ⓐ Ⓑ Ⓒ Ⓓ Ⓔ
3. Ⓐ Ⓑ Ⓒ Ⓓ Ⓔ   28. Ⓐ Ⓑ Ⓒ Ⓓ Ⓔ
4. Ⓐ Ⓑ Ⓒ Ⓓ Ⓔ   29. Ⓐ Ⓑ Ⓒ Ⓓ Ⓔ
5. Ⓐ Ⓑ Ⓒ Ⓓ Ⓔ   30. Ⓐ Ⓑ Ⓒ Ⓓ Ⓔ
6. Ⓐ Ⓑ Ⓒ Ⓓ Ⓔ   31. Ⓐ Ⓑ Ⓒ Ⓓ Ⓔ
7. Ⓐ Ⓑ Ⓒ Ⓓ Ⓔ   32. Ⓐ Ⓑ Ⓒ Ⓓ Ⓔ
8. Ⓐ Ⓑ Ⓒ Ⓓ Ⓔ   33. Ⓐ Ⓑ Ⓒ Ⓓ Ⓔ
9. Ⓐ Ⓑ Ⓒ Ⓓ Ⓔ   34. Ⓐ Ⓑ Ⓒ Ⓓ Ⓔ
10. Ⓐ Ⓑ Ⓒ Ⓓ Ⓔ   35. Ⓐ Ⓑ Ⓒ Ⓓ Ⓔ
11. Ⓐ Ⓑ Ⓒ Ⓓ Ⓔ   36. Ⓐ Ⓑ Ⓒ Ⓓ Ⓔ
12. Ⓐ Ⓑ Ⓒ Ⓓ Ⓔ   37. Ⓐ Ⓑ Ⓒ Ⓓ Ⓔ
13. Ⓐ Ⓑ Ⓒ Ⓓ Ⓔ   38. Ⓐ Ⓑ Ⓒ Ⓓ Ⓔ
14. Ⓐ Ⓑ Ⓒ Ⓓ Ⓔ   39. Ⓐ Ⓑ Ⓒ Ⓓ Ⓔ
15. Ⓐ Ⓑ Ⓒ Ⓓ Ⓔ   40. Ⓐ Ⓑ Ⓒ Ⓓ Ⓔ
16. Ⓐ Ⓑ Ⓒ Ⓓ Ⓔ   41. Ⓐ Ⓑ Ⓒ Ⓓ Ⓔ
17. Ⓐ Ⓑ Ⓒ Ⓓ Ⓔ   42. Ⓐ Ⓑ Ⓒ Ⓓ Ⓔ
18. Ⓐ Ⓑ Ⓒ Ⓓ Ⓔ   43. Ⓐ Ⓑ Ⓒ Ⓓ Ⓔ
19. Ⓐ Ⓑ Ⓒ Ⓓ Ⓔ   44. Ⓐ Ⓑ Ⓒ Ⓓ Ⓔ
20. Ⓐ Ⓑ Ⓒ Ⓓ Ⓔ   45. Ⓐ Ⓑ Ⓒ Ⓓ Ⓔ
21. Ⓐ Ⓑ Ⓒ Ⓓ Ⓔ   46. Ⓐ Ⓑ Ⓒ Ⓓ Ⓔ
22. Ⓐ Ⓑ Ⓒ Ⓓ Ⓔ   47. Ⓐ Ⓑ Ⓒ Ⓓ Ⓔ
23. Ⓐ Ⓑ Ⓒ Ⓓ Ⓔ   48. Ⓐ Ⓑ Ⓒ Ⓓ Ⓔ
24. Ⓐ Ⓑ Ⓒ Ⓓ Ⓔ   49. Ⓐ Ⓑ Ⓒ Ⓓ Ⓔ
25. Ⓐ Ⓑ Ⓒ Ⓓ Ⓔ   50. Ⓐ Ⓑ Ⓒ Ⓓ Ⓔ

SAT Math Level 1

Practice Test 3

1. Ⓐ Ⓑ Ⓒ Ⓓ Ⓔ	26. Ⓐ Ⓑ Ⓒ Ⓓ Ⓔ
2. Ⓐ Ⓑ Ⓒ Ⓓ Ⓔ	27. Ⓐ Ⓑ Ⓒ Ⓓ Ⓔ
3. Ⓐ Ⓑ Ⓒ Ⓓ Ⓔ	28. Ⓐ Ⓑ Ⓒ Ⓓ Ⓔ
4. Ⓐ Ⓑ Ⓒ Ⓓ Ⓔ	29. Ⓐ Ⓑ Ⓒ Ⓓ Ⓔ
5. Ⓐ Ⓑ Ⓒ Ⓓ Ⓔ	30. Ⓐ Ⓑ Ⓒ Ⓓ Ⓔ
6. Ⓐ Ⓑ Ⓒ Ⓓ Ⓔ	31. Ⓐ Ⓑ Ⓒ Ⓓ Ⓔ
7. Ⓐ Ⓑ Ⓒ Ⓓ Ⓔ	32. Ⓐ Ⓑ Ⓒ Ⓓ Ⓔ
8. Ⓐ Ⓑ Ⓒ Ⓓ Ⓔ	33. Ⓐ Ⓑ Ⓒ Ⓓ Ⓔ
9. Ⓐ Ⓑ Ⓒ Ⓓ Ⓔ	34. Ⓐ Ⓑ Ⓒ Ⓓ Ⓔ
10. Ⓐ Ⓑ Ⓒ Ⓓ Ⓔ	35. Ⓐ Ⓑ Ⓒ Ⓓ Ⓔ
11. Ⓐ Ⓑ Ⓒ Ⓓ Ⓔ	36. Ⓐ Ⓑ Ⓒ Ⓓ Ⓔ
12. Ⓐ Ⓑ Ⓒ Ⓓ Ⓔ	37. Ⓐ Ⓑ Ⓒ Ⓓ Ⓔ
13. Ⓐ Ⓑ Ⓒ Ⓓ Ⓔ	38. Ⓐ Ⓑ Ⓒ Ⓓ Ⓔ
14. Ⓐ Ⓑ Ⓒ Ⓓ Ⓔ	39. Ⓐ Ⓑ Ⓒ Ⓓ Ⓔ
15. Ⓐ Ⓑ Ⓒ Ⓓ Ⓔ	40. Ⓐ Ⓑ Ⓒ Ⓓ Ⓔ
16. Ⓐ Ⓑ Ⓒ Ⓓ Ⓔ	41. Ⓐ Ⓑ Ⓒ Ⓓ Ⓔ
17. Ⓐ Ⓑ Ⓒ Ⓓ Ⓔ	42. Ⓐ Ⓑ Ⓒ Ⓓ Ⓔ
18. Ⓐ Ⓑ Ⓒ Ⓓ Ⓔ	43. Ⓐ Ⓑ Ⓒ Ⓓ Ⓔ
19. Ⓐ Ⓑ Ⓒ Ⓓ Ⓔ	44. Ⓐ Ⓑ Ⓒ Ⓓ Ⓔ
20. Ⓐ Ⓑ Ⓒ Ⓓ Ⓔ	45. Ⓐ Ⓑ Ⓒ Ⓓ Ⓔ
21. Ⓐ Ⓑ Ⓒ Ⓓ Ⓔ	46. Ⓐ Ⓑ Ⓒ Ⓓ Ⓔ
22. Ⓐ Ⓑ Ⓒ Ⓓ Ⓔ	47. Ⓐ Ⓑ Ⓒ Ⓓ Ⓔ
23. Ⓐ Ⓑ Ⓒ Ⓓ Ⓔ	48. Ⓐ Ⓑ Ⓒ Ⓓ Ⓔ
24. Ⓐ Ⓑ Ⓒ Ⓓ Ⓔ	49. Ⓐ Ⓑ Ⓒ Ⓓ Ⓔ
25. Ⓐ Ⓑ Ⓒ Ⓓ Ⓔ	50. Ⓐ Ⓑ Ⓒ Ⓓ Ⓔ

SAT Math Level 1

Practice Test 4

1. Ⓐ Ⓑ Ⓒ Ⓓ Ⓔ
2. Ⓐ Ⓑ Ⓒ Ⓓ Ⓔ
3. Ⓐ Ⓑ Ⓒ Ⓓ Ⓔ
4. Ⓐ Ⓑ Ⓒ Ⓓ Ⓔ
5. Ⓐ Ⓑ Ⓒ Ⓓ Ⓔ
6. Ⓐ Ⓑ Ⓒ Ⓓ Ⓔ
7. Ⓐ Ⓑ Ⓒ Ⓓ Ⓔ
8. Ⓐ Ⓑ Ⓒ Ⓓ Ⓔ
9. Ⓐ Ⓑ Ⓒ Ⓓ Ⓔ
10. Ⓐ Ⓑ Ⓒ Ⓓ Ⓔ
11. Ⓐ Ⓑ Ⓒ Ⓓ Ⓔ
12. Ⓐ Ⓑ Ⓒ Ⓓ Ⓔ
13. Ⓐ Ⓑ Ⓒ Ⓓ Ⓔ
14. Ⓐ Ⓑ Ⓒ Ⓓ Ⓔ
15. Ⓐ Ⓑ Ⓒ Ⓓ Ⓔ
16. Ⓐ Ⓑ Ⓒ Ⓓ Ⓔ
17. Ⓐ Ⓑ Ⓒ Ⓓ Ⓔ
18. Ⓐ Ⓑ Ⓒ Ⓓ Ⓔ
19. Ⓐ Ⓑ Ⓒ Ⓓ Ⓔ
20. Ⓐ Ⓑ Ⓒ Ⓓ Ⓔ
21. Ⓐ Ⓑ Ⓒ Ⓓ Ⓔ
22. Ⓐ Ⓑ Ⓒ Ⓓ Ⓔ
23. Ⓐ Ⓑ Ⓒ Ⓓ Ⓔ
24. Ⓐ Ⓑ Ⓒ Ⓓ Ⓔ
25. Ⓐ Ⓑ Ⓒ Ⓓ Ⓔ

26. Ⓐ Ⓑ Ⓒ Ⓓ Ⓔ
27. Ⓐ Ⓑ Ⓒ Ⓓ Ⓔ
28. Ⓐ Ⓑ Ⓒ Ⓓ Ⓔ
29. Ⓐ Ⓑ Ⓒ Ⓓ Ⓔ
30. Ⓐ Ⓑ Ⓒ Ⓓ Ⓔ
31. Ⓐ Ⓑ Ⓒ Ⓓ Ⓔ
32. Ⓐ Ⓑ Ⓒ Ⓓ Ⓔ
33. Ⓐ Ⓑ Ⓒ Ⓓ Ⓔ
34. Ⓐ Ⓑ Ⓒ Ⓓ Ⓔ
35. Ⓐ Ⓑ Ⓒ Ⓓ Ⓔ
36. Ⓐ Ⓑ Ⓒ Ⓓ Ⓔ
37. Ⓐ Ⓑ Ⓒ Ⓓ Ⓔ
38. Ⓐ Ⓑ Ⓒ Ⓓ Ⓔ
39. Ⓐ Ⓑ Ⓒ Ⓓ Ⓔ
40. Ⓐ Ⓑ Ⓒ Ⓓ Ⓔ
41. Ⓐ Ⓑ Ⓒ Ⓓ Ⓔ
42. Ⓐ Ⓑ Ⓒ Ⓓ Ⓔ
43. Ⓐ Ⓑ Ⓒ Ⓓ Ⓔ
44. Ⓐ Ⓑ Ⓒ Ⓓ Ⓔ
45. Ⓐ Ⓑ Ⓒ Ⓓ Ⓔ
46. Ⓐ Ⓑ Ⓒ Ⓓ Ⓔ
47. Ⓐ Ⓑ Ⓒ Ⓓ Ⓔ
48. Ⓐ Ⓑ Ⓒ Ⓓ Ⓔ
49. Ⓐ Ⓑ Ⓒ Ⓓ Ⓔ
50. Ⓐ Ⓑ Ⓒ Ⓓ Ⓔ

SAT Math Level 1

Practice Test 5

1. Ⓐ Ⓑ Ⓒ Ⓓ Ⓔ
2. Ⓐ Ⓑ Ⓒ Ⓓ Ⓔ
3. Ⓐ Ⓑ Ⓒ Ⓓ Ⓔ
4. Ⓐ Ⓑ Ⓒ Ⓓ Ⓔ
5. Ⓐ Ⓑ Ⓒ Ⓓ Ⓔ
6. Ⓐ Ⓑ Ⓒ Ⓓ Ⓔ
7. Ⓐ Ⓑ Ⓒ Ⓓ Ⓔ
8. Ⓐ Ⓑ Ⓒ Ⓓ Ⓔ
9. Ⓐ Ⓑ Ⓒ Ⓓ Ⓔ
10. Ⓐ Ⓑ Ⓒ Ⓓ Ⓔ
11. Ⓐ Ⓑ Ⓒ Ⓓ Ⓔ
12. Ⓐ Ⓑ Ⓒ Ⓓ Ⓔ
13. Ⓐ Ⓑ Ⓒ Ⓓ Ⓔ
14. Ⓐ Ⓑ Ⓒ Ⓓ Ⓔ
15. Ⓐ Ⓑ Ⓒ Ⓓ Ⓔ
16. Ⓐ Ⓑ Ⓒ Ⓓ Ⓔ
17. Ⓐ Ⓑ Ⓒ Ⓓ Ⓔ
18. Ⓐ Ⓑ Ⓒ Ⓓ Ⓔ
19. Ⓐ Ⓑ Ⓒ Ⓓ Ⓔ
20. Ⓐ Ⓑ Ⓒ Ⓓ Ⓔ
21. Ⓐ Ⓑ Ⓒ Ⓓ Ⓔ
22. Ⓐ Ⓑ Ⓒ Ⓓ Ⓔ
23. Ⓐ Ⓑ Ⓒ Ⓓ Ⓔ
24. Ⓐ Ⓑ Ⓒ Ⓓ Ⓔ
25. Ⓐ Ⓑ Ⓒ Ⓓ Ⓔ

26. Ⓐ Ⓑ Ⓒ Ⓓ Ⓔ
27. Ⓐ Ⓑ Ⓒ Ⓓ Ⓔ
28. Ⓐ Ⓑ Ⓒ Ⓓ Ⓔ
29. Ⓐ Ⓑ Ⓒ Ⓓ Ⓔ
30. Ⓐ Ⓑ Ⓒ Ⓓ Ⓔ
31. Ⓐ Ⓑ Ⓒ Ⓓ Ⓔ
32. Ⓐ Ⓑ Ⓒ Ⓓ Ⓔ
33. Ⓐ Ⓑ Ⓒ Ⓓ Ⓔ
34. Ⓐ Ⓑ Ⓒ Ⓓ Ⓔ
35. Ⓐ Ⓑ Ⓒ Ⓓ Ⓔ
36. Ⓐ Ⓑ Ⓒ Ⓓ Ⓔ
37. Ⓐ Ⓑ Ⓒ Ⓓ Ⓔ
38. Ⓐ Ⓑ Ⓒ Ⓓ Ⓔ
39. Ⓐ Ⓑ Ⓒ Ⓓ Ⓔ
40. Ⓐ Ⓑ Ⓒ Ⓓ Ⓔ
41. Ⓐ Ⓑ Ⓒ Ⓓ Ⓔ
42. Ⓐ Ⓑ Ⓒ Ⓓ Ⓔ
43. Ⓐ Ⓑ Ⓒ Ⓓ Ⓔ
44. Ⓐ Ⓑ Ⓒ Ⓓ Ⓔ
45. Ⓐ Ⓑ Ⓒ Ⓓ Ⓔ
46. Ⓐ Ⓑ Ⓒ Ⓓ Ⓔ
47. Ⓐ Ⓑ Ⓒ Ⓓ Ⓔ
48. Ⓐ Ⓑ Ⓒ Ⓓ Ⓔ
49. Ⓐ Ⓑ Ⓒ Ⓓ Ⓔ
50. Ⓐ Ⓑ Ⓒ Ⓓ Ⓔ

SAT Math Level 1

Practice Test 6

1. Ⓐ Ⓑ Ⓒ Ⓓ Ⓔ
2. Ⓐ Ⓑ Ⓒ Ⓓ Ⓔ
3. Ⓐ Ⓑ Ⓒ Ⓓ Ⓔ
4. Ⓐ Ⓑ Ⓒ Ⓓ Ⓔ
5. Ⓐ Ⓑ Ⓒ Ⓓ Ⓔ
6. Ⓐ Ⓑ Ⓒ Ⓓ Ⓔ
7. Ⓐ Ⓑ Ⓒ Ⓓ Ⓔ
8. Ⓐ Ⓑ Ⓒ Ⓓ Ⓔ
9. Ⓐ Ⓑ Ⓒ Ⓓ Ⓔ
10. Ⓐ Ⓑ Ⓒ Ⓓ Ⓔ
11. Ⓐ Ⓑ Ⓒ Ⓓ Ⓔ
12. Ⓐ Ⓑ Ⓒ Ⓓ Ⓔ
13. Ⓐ Ⓑ Ⓒ Ⓓ Ⓔ
14. Ⓐ Ⓑ Ⓒ Ⓓ Ⓔ
15. Ⓐ Ⓑ Ⓒ Ⓓ Ⓔ
16. Ⓐ Ⓑ Ⓒ Ⓓ Ⓔ
17. Ⓐ Ⓑ Ⓒ Ⓓ Ⓔ
18. Ⓐ Ⓑ Ⓒ Ⓓ Ⓔ
19. Ⓐ Ⓑ Ⓒ Ⓓ Ⓔ
20. Ⓐ Ⓑ Ⓒ Ⓓ Ⓔ
21. Ⓐ Ⓑ Ⓒ Ⓓ Ⓔ
22. Ⓐ Ⓑ Ⓒ Ⓓ Ⓔ
23. Ⓐ Ⓑ Ⓒ Ⓓ Ⓔ
24. Ⓐ Ⓑ Ⓒ Ⓓ Ⓔ
25. Ⓐ Ⓑ Ⓒ Ⓓ Ⓔ

26. Ⓐ Ⓑ Ⓒ Ⓓ Ⓔ
27. Ⓐ Ⓑ Ⓒ Ⓓ Ⓔ
28. Ⓐ Ⓑ Ⓒ Ⓓ Ⓔ
29. Ⓐ Ⓑ Ⓒ Ⓓ Ⓔ
30. Ⓐ Ⓑ Ⓒ Ⓓ Ⓔ
31. Ⓐ Ⓑ Ⓒ Ⓓ Ⓔ
32. Ⓐ Ⓑ Ⓒ Ⓓ Ⓔ
33. Ⓐ Ⓑ Ⓒ Ⓓ Ⓔ
34. Ⓐ Ⓑ Ⓒ Ⓓ Ⓔ
35. Ⓐ Ⓑ Ⓒ Ⓓ Ⓔ
36. Ⓐ Ⓑ Ⓒ Ⓓ Ⓔ
37. Ⓐ Ⓑ Ⓒ Ⓓ Ⓔ
38. Ⓐ Ⓑ Ⓒ Ⓓ Ⓔ
39. Ⓐ Ⓑ Ⓒ Ⓓ Ⓔ
40. Ⓐ Ⓑ Ⓒ Ⓓ Ⓔ
41. Ⓐ Ⓑ Ⓒ Ⓓ Ⓔ
42. Ⓐ Ⓑ Ⓒ Ⓓ Ⓔ
43. Ⓐ Ⓑ Ⓒ Ⓓ Ⓔ
44. Ⓐ Ⓑ Ⓒ Ⓓ Ⓔ
45. Ⓐ Ⓑ Ⓒ Ⓓ Ⓔ
46. Ⓐ Ⓑ Ⓒ Ⓓ Ⓔ
47. Ⓐ Ⓑ Ⓒ Ⓓ Ⓔ
48. Ⓐ Ⓑ Ⓒ Ⓓ Ⓔ
49. Ⓐ Ⓑ Ⓒ Ⓓ Ⓔ
50. Ⓐ Ⓑ Ⓒ Ⓓ Ⓔ

REA's Test Prep Books Are The Best!

(a sample of the <u>hundreds of letters</u> REA receives each year)

" I am writing to congratulate you on preparing an exceptional study guide. In five years of teaching this course I have never encountered a more thorough, comprehensive, concise and realistic preparation for this examination. "
Teacher, Davie, FL

" I have found your publications, *The Best Test Preparation...*, to be exactly that. "
Teacher, Aptos, CA

" I used your *CLEP Introductory Sociology* book and rank it 99% — thank you! "
Student, Jerusalem, Israel

" Your *GMAT* book greatly helped me on the test. Thank you. "
Student, Oxford, OH

" I recently got the *French SAT II* Exam book from REA. I congratulate you on first-rate French practice tests."
Instructor, Los Angeles, CA

" Your *AP English Literature and Composition* book is most impressive."
Student, Montgomery, AL

" The REA *LSAT* Test Preparation guide is a winner! "
Instructor, Spartanburg, SC